Freedom from Brokenness

"So many people live in bondage even though Jesus said He came to set us free. My friend, Gena Barnhill, offers a wonderful resource that will help so many people throw off the chains of bondage and enjoy God's freedom through healing prayer. Her personal stories and practical guidance will make this book a useful resource for prayer ministries and a helpful tool for personal, spiritual victory."

TIM RIORDAN,
Pastor, SonRise Baptist Church, Newnan, GA, and author of 14 books

"If you've ever wondered why you can't seem to shake the past or you feel stuck in your present sin with its subsequent guilt, shame, and frustration, then you have your hands on the possible answer. Gena has written a very practical and hopeful book that will not only educate and guide you through the steps to healing, but it's also backed with years of proven success with people just like you. No need to live in bondage any longer."

RICK OUIMET,
Founder and President of Straight Street Ministries,
Founding Pastor of Mosaic Lynchburg

"In *Freedom from Brokenness*, Gena Barnhill manages to gently but thoroughly get to the heart of a most important spiritual matter for every Christian. She gets to the root of Satan's deception and how he likes to think our history, our here-and-now, and our future is somehow his playground. But she also shows us how to obtain freedom from such in Jesus's name—how we can both find it and embrace it. *Freedom from Brokenness* reminds us that nothing and no one can separate us from God's love and from His ultimate plan for our life. This should be a must-read for every Christian!"

EVA MARIE EVERSON,
President of Word Weavers International,
multi award-winning author and speaker

"Gena Barnhill's *Freedom from Brokenness* delivers on its title. This is that rare book on the healing of the heart: distilled, easy-to-understand key principles in clear language; strong biblical foundations for them; and real-world stories illustrating each idea in a way that increases faith in God's goodness. The Barnhills have both lived out and ministered the truths of this book. Whether you are seeking this freedom for yourself for the first time or feel called to help others the way Jesus has helped you, you have in your hands a reliable compass from a trustworthy guide."

TOM HOLLOWAY,
Asst. Dir. Global School of Supernatural Ministry

FREEDOM

from

BROKENNESS

Lessons Learned

through

Inner Healing Prayer

Gena Barnhill

Birmingham, Alabama
Freedom from Brokenness

[Brookstone Publishing Group]
An imprint of Iron Stream Media
100 Missionary Ridge
Birmingham, AL 35242
IronStreamMedia.com

Library of Congress Control Number: 2022900799

Cover design by Melinda Martin

ISBN: 978-1-949856-52-1 (paperback)
ISBN: 978-1-949856-53-8 (e-book)

1 2 3 4 5—25 24 23 22 21

MANUFACTURED IN THE UNITED STATES OF AMERICA

DEDICATION

This book is gratefully dedicated to each of the people we prayed with for inner healing. Watching the Holy Spirit heal your hearts increased our faith in the Lord and blessed us beyond measure. Although your names were changed to protect your identity, the Lord knows you and will never leave you. We continue to lift you up in prayer in your journey to wholeness.

Contents

Acknowledgments

To Pat Fitzgibbons, who provided the initial opportunity to learn about inner healing prayer and walked alongside Press and me as we taught and prayed with others.

To all the people who graciously allowed Press and I to pray with them for healing, I thank you. Watching the Holy Spirit heal you blessed us more than you know.

To the phenomenal team at Brookstone Publishing Group, I could not get through this without your support and encouragement.

Introduction

Have you ever wished you could leave your past behind? Completely erase it and start over? You can.

Your past does not need to define you. Nor is your identity based on previous mistakes you made, or on the identity others may have tried to place on you, or on the identity you created for yourself based on life experiences. Jesus can wipe your slate clean and give you a new start when you anchor your identity in Him.

I did not fully understand this until my mid-fifties, when an encounter with the Holy Spirit at an inner healing prayer conference changed my life. Although I was a Christian, I'd never experienced this before. I learned the Lord wants to heal our deep emotional suffering and painful memories. Through the inner healing prayer process, Jesus removes layers of our woundedness, similar to how we peel layers of an onion. He can reach into a person's life and transform their memories with His restoring presence. Sometimes this happens right away. Other times, over a period of time. Like most things in life, each situation is different. In this book, I'll share the details and tell you how you, too, can experience the power, peace, and freedom many Christians are missing.

For as long as I can remember, even before my encounter, I felt drawn to helping people and understanding human behavior. In my life, I enjoyed introspection and analyzing my behavior to target areas where I needed improvement. I thought if I could figure out why I behaved the way I did, I could help others understand their behaviors. This reflective nature led me to pursue careers as a registered nurse, a counselor, and a school psychologist. In my mid-forties, I studied with autism experts and behavior analysts to help individuals on the autism spectrum and their families lead fulfilled lives.

I was driven by gaining knowledge, studying research, and learning from my past mistakes, as well as those of others. All this to become a better person. Even after gaining insight from voracious studying, a void remained in my life. No matter how hard I tried, periodic feelings of inadequacy plagued me.

Being a Christian, I was aware we serve a triune God composed of God the Father, Jesus the Son, and the Holy Spirit. I also knew human beings are composed of three parts: physical bodies, souls (our minds, will, and emotions), and spirits. I had an incomplete understanding of the Holy Spirit and the spirit realm until I was introduced to inner healing through Christian Healing Ministries (CHM).[1] I knew about the Holy Spirit, but I did not know Him personally. I also did not grasp the magnitude of unseen spiritual warfare and how it can negatively impact us.

After receiving my own inner healing through CHM, I felt called to the inner healing ministry. Attending training classes and conferences, and practicing the skills taught, were critical aspects of becoming a prayer minister. Given the years I spent in college academic programs, participating in these activities felt familiar—with a twist.

Unlike my past experiences in academia, a wonderful world of intimacy with the Holy Spirit opened for me. I received a deep awareness of His power that resides in me, like nothing I'd previously known. I no longer needed to struggle to navigate life or try to fill the void. Instead, I had a friend in the Holy Spirit who interceded and comforted me. No more striving. No more self-reliance. Instead, I learned how to rest in the Lord and enjoy His peace.

I believe God wants us to encounter more of Him while we are still here on earth. We do not need to wait until we get to Heaven to experience more power, joy, and revelation from the Lord. It is my heart's desire for others, which includes you, to experience the richness the Lord has for each person while here on earth.

Randy Clark's *There is More! The Secret to Experiencing God's Power to Change Your Life* clearly describes the more God has for us in our current earthly life.[2] Inner healing prayer opened the door to God's truth about my destiny and purpose, something I had not clearly understood. The Holy Spirit filled the emptiness and provided direction and guidance when I sought Him in prayer and daily conversation.

My husband, Press, and I have been actively involved in inner healing prayer ministry in our community and church for more than ten years. We also prayed weekly in a men's prison ministry for several years until the COVID-19 pandemic struck. The men voluntarily signed up for prayer appointments through the chaplains. Many accounts of the healing experiences and the freedom we saw when we prayed with others are interwoven throughout this book to inspire the reader.

In fall 2019, Press sensed the Lord's urging to write a manual to simply describe the fundamental principles we learned in our training and ministry practice. We wanted to provide a resource so people could implement these tenets and partner with the Holy Spirit to enact freedom from burdens. The Bible is clear: the Lord wants to set the captives free. Press sensed this manual should be called *Simple Effective Prayer: A Model for Inner Healing*, or SEP.

Initially, I questioned the need for another instruction book since excellent resources already existed. After praying, Press and I both believed we were to write a concise guidebook that described the principles we learned, especially from the prison ministry. We completed the first draft of *Simple Effective Prayer: A Model for Inner Healing* in January 2020. The following month, we trained people at our church who expressed an interest in becoming prayer ministers following the SEP method. We revised the manual in 2021 to reflect new insights gained through praying with others throughout the year.

This book is an extension of *Simple Effective Prayer: A Model for Inner Healing*. It provides spiritual and practical insights into how the Holy Spirit can repair heart wounds and guide a person to find their true identity in Christ. It goes beyond the basic principles provided in the original SEP message by elaborating on deeper concepts.

Inner healing is a process and often occurs over time. I hope by reading this book, you will be blessed and find healing and hope in your quest for peace and freedom. I want to share what the Lord has taught me so you can experience the Holy Spirit's presence like never before. Your inheritance in the Lord is something you can truly enjoy right now. You simply need to remain open and receive it. Then ask for a restart.

Blessings on your journey,

Gena Barnhill

SECTION 1

Darkness

Jesus came to heal the brokenhearted and set us free. For many people, the first step in breaking free is the awareness there is darkness around us, and we do have an enemy. If we remain ignorant of the enemy's temptation, deception, and accusation tactics, negative spirits of darkness can take hold. The good news is the Lord does not want us to fear the enemy or fall prey to evil. Instead, we are to take hold of Luke 10:19 and believe *all* who confess Jesus as their Lord and Savior have power and authority against these forces. Then we need to put on the full armor of God and exercise that power and authority over the enemy in Jesus's name.

Chapter 1

Darkness Can Take Hold, but Don't Fear

An invisible world exists all around us. Several hundred verses in the Bible describe angels as supernatural beings used by God to direct, encourage, protect, and instruct us. Hebrews 1:14 describes them as "ministering spirits sent out to serve for the sake of those who are to inherit salvation." The Bible shows where God used angels to deliver messages to His people, warn, bring healing and comfort, guard, and enlighten His children. Angels ministered to Jesus. But spiritual beings who serve God and His people are not the only ones who exist in another realm.

Supernatural entities who seek to inflict evil and wreak havoc in our lives also compete for our attention. These evil spirits include the fallen angel Satan and his agents. Sometimes these evil spirits are referred to in Christian writings as the devil, the enemy, or the thief. In this book, the enemy will refer to any evil spirit in the kingdom of darkness.

I grew up believing the devil was not real. Comedian Flip Wilson reinforced this belief when he jokingly told his audiences in the 1960s that the devil made him do things he should not have done. I was under the impression the devil was a fabricated excuse. I thought people used "the devil" to place blame outside themselves for something they did that caused shame or embarrassment. I had no idea he was an actual entity.

The churches I attended as a child, teen, and young adult did not discuss the devil, reinforcing my belief that he was not real. I later learned from pastor and author R. T. Kendall the devil prefers we disbelieve his existence. Kendall also claims that if you do not believe in Satan's reality, he already succeeded with you, because unbelief is his work.[1]

The Bible clearly states we have an enemy in the following two scriptures. 1 Peter 5:8 says, "Be sober-minded; be watchful. Your adversary the devil prowls around like a roaring lion, seeking someone to devour." Ephesians 6:12 says, "For we do not wrestle against flesh and blood, but against the rulers, against the authorities, against the cosmic powers over this present darkness, against the spiritual forces of evil in the heavenly places."

In my early fifties, other Christians I spoke with acknowledged the existence of evil spirits. They claimed they could not impact Christians because we have accepted Christ as our Savior. I believed this for about five years and assumed that dark forces could not influence me since I was a Christian. I did not understand evil influence certainly was possible until I attended healing prayer classes and learned how the enemy could negatively impact people.

Jesus refers to the devil as "the father of lies" in John 8:44. Our enemy lies to us about the nature and character of God, just as he did with Adam and Eve when he convinced them God withheld good from them. He lies about our relationship with God, convincing us we can never receive God's love and forgiveness because we are not worthy. The enemy also plants lies about others to bring offense, confusion, miscommunication, and separation among God's people.[2] When we believe Satan's lies, knowingly or unknowingly, we can feel oppressed, stressed, or tormented by our thoughts.

Frank Hammond, the late author of Christian books on deliverance and spiritual warfare, said the devil attacks us through three means: temptation, accusation, or deception.

Satan first tempted Jesus, knowing our Lord was hungry after forty days of fasting, by saying to Him if He was the Son of God, He should command the stones to become bread. Next, Satan tempted Jesus by telling Him to throw Himself down from the temple's pinnacle because the Scriptures indicated the Lord would give angels charge over Him for protection. Then the devil took Jesus up to a high mountain to show Him the world's kingdoms, and he promised them to Jesus if the Son of God promised to worship him. (See Matthew 4.)

Hammond further explains parallels between Jesus's temptations and the temptation of Eve in the Garden of Eden. In Jesus's first temptation and Eve's, the devil appealed to the lust of the flesh, and he also cast doubt on the Word of God. In their second temptations, the devil appealed to the pride of life with the offer of self-promotion. The devil used lust of the eyes to entice Jesus in the third temptation and to tempt Eve to accept the world's allure instead of God's will.[3]

Not every thought that comes into our mind is our own. The devil accuses and deceives us by planting lies, especially when we are vulnerable after a traumatic event or episode of depression, rejection, or loneliness. Physical exhaustion, hunger, and anger can leave us susceptible to the enemy's lies. Young children often lack the defenses to withstand the enemy's lies. If the devil can get us to believe a lie, he then gains influence in our lives. He has been watching our families for generations, and he knows our areas of vulnerability and weakness. He is stalking around, waiting for the right time to catch us off guard.

During my elementary school years, my mother often told me that she did not approve of something I said or did. I frequently replied I was sorry and would try harder to do better next time. I thought I sincerely apologized for my behavior and assumed I needed to work harder at avoiding the same mistake. My mother usually told me that my apology was "not enough."

Since my earnest reply was not considered sufficient, I assumed something was wrong with me. Unbeknownst to me at the time, I bought into the enemy's lie that I was flawed and inadequate. I thought I needed to strive and perform correctly in all situations to achieve value and acceptance. I sought the unattainable goal of perfection for the next forty years.

In my fifties, a healing prayer session revealed a performance-based mindset based on the mistaken belief that I was not good enough. I was not alone in this thinking. A number of relatives also believed they needed to strive and perform for acceptance.

People typically do not recognize the lies because they have been part of their thought processes and lineage for a long time. I believe the enemy used my mother's response that my apology was not enough to convince me I was not good enough and probably never would be.

The enemy also can use people other than a family, as well as situations, to reinforce our mistaken beliefs about ourselves and our identity. Perhaps you auditioned in a singing competition and were told you were the worst singer the judge ever heard. You then came to believe the lie that said, "You will never be a singer because you are a failure." This belief could have led you to expect you would fail at everything you attempt.

You also may have believed this propensity to fail is part of your personality and will never change because you embraced an identity of incompetence. Because you have become so familiar with these thoughts, you do not fathom they are lies of the enemy, designed to stop you from living out your God-given destiny. We are told the truth in Philippians 4:13, which says, "I can do all things through him, who strengthens me." If God has called you to something, He will see you through it because He always equips those He calls. He has given those who believe in Jesus Christ and call on His name the power of the Holy Spirit.

Those who believe in Jesus as their Savior have the power and authority to fight battles in Jesus's name. We do not need to fear the enemy because Jesus tells us in Luke 10:19, "Behold, I have given you authority to tread on serpents and scorpions, and over all the power of the enemy, and nothing shall hurt you." Jesus said in John 10:10, "The thief comes only to steal and kill and destroy. I came that they may have life and have it abundantly."

Jesus also can heal and bring restoration to any damage caused by the enemy and his agents. We just need to ask Him for this healing. In Zechariah 9:12, the Lord declared, "I will restore to you double." Press and I prayed with many people who told us God restored their broken relationships and gave them way more than they requested.

I have experienced that as well. I interviewed for a faculty position recommended by a colleague in 2003. She endorsed me as the ideal candidate for the job. After hours of interviews and faculty observations while I taught classes, the Department Chairperson offered me the job. Ecstatic over the new career opportunity, I could not wait to drive home to tell Press. We celebrated over dinner that evening, and we discussed our future. I mentioned to Press and my colleague that all the faculty members were encouraging and supportive except for one person. I sensed an uneasy atmosphere in the presence of that one faculty member. My colleague assured me that my concern was a non-issue, and the job was mine.

Two days later, the Department Chair called to say the job description changed, and he offered the position to another candidate. I hung up the phone, confused and disillusioned. Feelings of betrayal, disappointment, and anger surfaced. I could not understand why the Department Chair rescinded the job offer. Would I ever achieve my dream to teach full time at the university level? I questioned my competence and ability to teach, completely unaware that I had entertained lies from the enemy.

After praying about the situation, I received assurance from the Lord that He had a better plan. I did not know what that plan would look like or when it would happen. I wish I could say I held steadfast to the Lord's promise, but that was not always the case. From time to time, I became impatient and doubted my capabilities.

A few years later, I interviewed at a different university for a faculty position to design a new program to train teachers to work with students with autism. This job proved to be far better than I initially imagined. Opportunities to lead several research projects, publish journal articles, and create additional academic coursework blessed me beyond my expectations. Although the disappointment over losing the other faculty position was gone, I remained ignorant of the enemy's tactics and his influence in my life.

We need to be aware of how the enemy operates so we do not allow him and his agents to keep us from the fullness of God's purpose in our lives. When we are ignorant of the enemy's existence, he controls more of our lives than we realize.

He is subtle and influences our mindsets to form attitudes about ourselves and others. Lack of empathy and love for others may result. We could be unaware of the emotional baggage we carry. The enemy would have been pleased if I continued to justify my anger over how the first job offer was mishandled and stayed locked in bitterness. I would have missed the better opportunity if I had wallowed in this emotional pain. The new faculty position necessitated a move to another state where I met people who introduced me to inner healing prayer five years later.

Even though I professed to be a Christian and was active in church work for many years, I was unaware of the power and authority I possessed in Jesus Christ until my fifties. The enemy must have been exceptionally pleased with my ignorance of this power and authority because, practically speaking, I was an ineffective Christian. I did not recognize that I could partner with the Holy Spirit for healing and command evil spirits to leave and stop oppressing God's people. I had not taken hold of what Jesus said in Luke 10:19 for myself, until I learned about inner healing prayer and received the Baptism of the Holy Spirit.

Inner healing touches the most profound areas of pain in our hearts and minds when we allow the Lord to heal these areas. He removes layers of wounding and transforms painful memories. I learned from multiple sources that we become wounded because of living in a fallen world where we all experience suffering, sin, and illness. Others inflict hurts on us, and we can wound ourselves. Yet, God can restore what the enemy stole even if darkness gained access.

The Holy Spirit dramatically got my attention in 2011 when Press and I attended our first inner healing conference called "The Abba's Heart: Living in the Love of the Father" in Herndon, Virginia.

Judith MacNutt, co-founder of CHM, said that Father God longs for a close, personal relationship with each of us, but many times we have the wrong image of God. We mistakenly expect Him to be angry and disappointed in us when this is not His true nature. If our earthly fathers, or those in authority over us, were angry and critical, we may attribute these characteristics to Father God. This mindset creates a hurdle in people's lives and causes them to distrust God.

Judith asked us to bow our heads and close our eyes while she spoke and prayed for the audience. She said many in the audience had a pain in their heart from wounding that resulted from an angry parent, alcoholism, abuse, rejection, mental illness in the family, poverty, or abandonment. I felt a stabbing pain in my heart like nothing I ever experienced before. Then Judith said the Lord wants to heal our inner wounds. The pain immediately subsided. She continued to speak and described God's fervent desire to love His children as a daddy. My body shook while I quietly sat in my seat.

Judith then described how Jesus healed a young boy and his sister after they experienced several traumatic events. Judith emphatically exclaimed Jesus desires to do the same for each person in the audience. At that point, I saw in my mind's eye a childhood memory, and the Lord showed me aspects of the situation I had misinterpreted. I thought it was my responsibility to defend my brother when my father raged at him. Instead, I fled to my room. The enemy caused me to believe some lies about myself and my identity. Jesus showed me that I had not failed my brother, and it was not my responsibility to save my brother from harm. He revealed He protected my brother and me, and the Holy Spirit never left us.

An overwhelming sense of peace and love flooded over me—something I'd never felt before. This experience marked the beginning of an intimate relationship with the Holy Spirit and a desire to know Him better.

We need to believe the Lord will protect us and stay close to Him in prayer and daily communication. We have no reason to despair or to become immobilized with fear concerning the enemy because Jesus rescued us from the tyranny of darkness. Paul tells us in Colossians 1:13–14, "He has delivered us from the domain of darkness and transferred us to the kingdom of his beloved Son, in whom we have redemption, the forgiveness of sins."

Paul also tells us in Ephesians 6:11: "Put on the whole armor of God, that you may be able to stand against the schemes of the devil." Paul's reference to the whole armor is a metaphor for the first-century Roman soldier's armor and battle dress. The armor metaphor tells the reader we are currently involved in an active spiritual battle.[4] We still need to put on the full armor of God for protection daily that Paul writes about in Ephesians 6:14–18.

Pray this prayer aloud adapted from Ephesians 6:14–18:

> I choose to be strong in the Lord, in the power of His might. I choose to put on the whole armor of God so I might stand against the methods of the enemy. I put on the breastplate of righteousness—the Lord Jesus Christ. I am righteous in Him. I put on the belt of truth and refuse deception. My feet are fitted with readiness that comes from the gospel of peace. I put on the helmet of salvation that covers and protects my mind and my outlook. I stand in the wisdom of Christ alone. I take up the shield of faith. I am covered from head to toe, so Satan's fiery darts cannot touch me. I take the sword of the Spirit, the Word of God, declaring it to be true, without error, reliable, powerful, and alive. Now I am dressed from head to foot with Christ. I pray in the Spirit on all occasions. Amen.

SECTION 2

Open Doors

Stopping the enemy begins by first recognizing an open door. Then repent for any part you may have played in opening that door or allowing it to remain open. You may need to repent on behalf of your ancestors who gave the enemy access. Ask for forgiveness and then receive the Holy Spirit's blessings.

Open doors to the enemy can include:

- Justifying or agreeing with sin
- Traumatic events and resulting lies
- Unforgiveness
- Negative ancestral influences or generational curses
- Word curses
- Any occult involvement
- Involvement in false belief systems, cults, and secret societies
- Contact with unholy things
- Unhealthy soul ties

CHAPTER 2

Sin, Trauma, and Unforgiveness

O pen doors or access points allow negative influences or darkness into our lives. These openings may have occurred before a person became a Christian, when they unknowingly let these influences in their lives. Even before we were born, our ancestors' behaviors may have given the enemy access to our lineage. It's important that we identify these entry points where our ancestors or we may have made agreements, knowingly or unknowingly, to partner with the enemy. These connections need to be broken to experience the Lord's freedom.

Personal sin is one way darkness can enter a person's life. Jake Kail, the lead pastor at Threshold Church, reminds us that sin is also an agreement with Satan.[1] The fundamental principle of wrongdoing is an agreement with the devil, allowing him admission to our lives.

The person who justifies, embraces, minimizes, or hides their sin, and does not ask for forgiveness, comes into agreement with the enemy, thus allowing him access. James 4:17 says anyone who knows to do good and does not do good sins. Rick Warren asserts that the root of all sin is failing to give God glory, and sin is adoring anything else more than God.[2]

We also are told in Ephesians 4:26–27: "Be angry and do not sin; do not let the sun go down on your anger, and give no opportunity to the devil." Anger is not a sin, but when we allow it to fester and embrace it, anger can become sin and give the devil a foothold.

I admit I have gone to bed angry, refusing to talk, or consider forgiving the person who offended me. I held on to my anger, hoping it would punish that person. I judged the individual who upset me and then used that judgment to defend my reaction to say unkind words or slam the door and refuse to talk. I thought I was right, and the other person was wrong and deserved my self-righteous anger. I did not recognize that I did not have the right to adjudicate. I endured suffering instead of the person who offended me.

I allowed the enemy a foothold and then started to believe his lies about me, the offender, and the situation. If there had not been evidence of sin before the offense to allow the enemy admittance into my life, I opened the door to darkness when I agreed with his lies.

Sin does not need to keep us in bondage. The simple solution is to confess our sin and repent (change our way or direction), and then the Lord promises to forgive us. 1 John 1:9 states, "If we confess our sins, he is faithful and just to forgive us our sins and to cleanse us from all unrighteousness."

Traumatic events and resulting lies are other ways darkness can enter a person's life. In these instances, the individual did not sin, but someone sinned against them. Examples of this include sexual, physical, verbal, and emotional abuse. Abuse is incredibly unjust, but the enemy does not play fair. In a moment of weakness resulting from the trauma, the person may agree with the enemy's lies, thinking they have no value, deserve the mistreatment, or are responsible for the exploitation.

Press and I prayed with a woman who believed God allowed her assault to teach her a lesson. This belief was a lie of the enemy. We asked her if she would like to invite the Lord into that traumatic memory during an inner healing prayer session. She said, "Yes." With closed eyes, she asked Jesus to show her where He was during the attack. She said she saw Him in her mind's eye standing near her, although she had been unaware of His presence at the time of the attack. She asked Jesus questions and told us what she sensed He said and did. Jesus indicated He was sad for her pain, and the attack was not His plan. He showed her that He protected her from fatal harm in that situation. Jesus did not set her up for punishment or to learn a lesson as she previously believed. The perpetrator later gave his life to the Lord, following her prayers for his salvation.

People often try to make sense of why trauma or tragedy occurs, and yet there are no easy answers as to why. We have heard Christian leaders say we live in a fallen world where people have free will and choose to make mistakes, allowing evil and chaos to reign. Unfortunately, sometimes people succumb to the chaos and evil in the world and hurt and assault others. Another explanation offered is that trauma is a spiritual attack from the enemy. We see Job and Peter's stories in the Bible where the Lord allowed an attack, and they both became spiritually stronger and richly blessed by the Lord. Others suggest suffering is a result of God's discipline.

Sharon Jaynes, author of *I'm Not Good Enough,* warns us not to be too quick to assume tragedy occurred because of something we did that deserves punishment. She points out that when God disciplined people in the Bible, such as Ananias and Sapphira, they knew exactly why they were being chastised and were not repentant.[3] The key to repentance is a contrite heart and a change of ways. The good news is the Bible assures us God quickly forgives when we repent and ask for forgiveness, and He remembers our sins no more.

When we don't repent for our mistakes, the enemy gains a foothold to wreak havoc in our lives. He reminds us of our errors and torments us with lies and accusations. In my own life, the enemy prompted me to recall harsh words I had said to someone. I rehearsed that interaction over and over in my mind and allowed the enemy to convince me I was mean-spirited and would never change. Several days later I apologized to the person and asked the Lord to forgive me and close the open door.

In addition to various types of abuse, the enemy can use other traumatic events to reinforce these lies. Challenging situations can include a difficult divorce, a death, a life-threatening or terminal illness, a natural disaster, a job loss, or a serious accident. The enemy uses these times of susceptibility and vulnerability to plant lies.

People may believe lies, such as they will always be victims, no one will ever like them, God does not love them, they deserve punishment, or life is hopeless in response to a traumatic event. A person whose spouse divorced them after screaming disparaging statements about their character, calling them incompetent, boring, and useless, may believe the lie they will never be loved.

The enemy is the master of deception. Ignorance of the enemy's ploys can allow his deceptions to take hold in our lives. Often, he takes a kernel of truth and twists it into a lie. That same spouse may have mishandled one situation at work and lost a business opportunity because they missed the application deadline. The enemy can use the missed deadline to plant the lie that they are incompetent. Believing their identity is rooted in incompetence seems plausible because they failed to meet the application closing date. The lie is the belief that this makes that person an incompetent one.

The enemy's ploys with children are particularly disturbing. He plays unfairly with youngsters who have not developed safeguards against his attacks. Derek Prince, the late Bible teacher and author, stated these attacks are particularly problematic in broken homes where bitter conflict is prevalent and the parents do not have time for their children. He believed this provides an environment that invites the presence of the enemy. Many young children do not have the needed emotional and spiritual defenses to handle the pressures associated with darkness.[4]

Prince believed spirits of "rejection, anger, fear, rebellion, misery, loneliness, depression and sometimes suicide" commonly exploit children.[5] Children who have experienced abuse may believe they were responsible for enticing their perpetrators. The truth is, children are never responsible for the actions of an abusive adult.

In addition to the traumatic events inflicted by others, youngsters can develop a spirit of fear from watching horror movies, video games, or being exposed to violence or pornography. This introduction can happen in homes with good parents who were never aware of their child's activities while at someone else's home or in another environment. Despite parents' best efforts, this exposure can happen in their own home.

In a surprise to many, trauma can occur prenatally and during the birth process. CHM training classes provided opportunities to observe trained prayer ministers praying for volunteers from the audience. While one volunteer explained her desire to be free from fear and anxiety during an inner healing prayer demonstration, she became aware her mother tried to abort her when pregnant.

The Lord revealed this was the root of her current emotional wounding. Tears streamed down her contorted face as a result of this revelation. Rather than continue the prayer demonstration in front of the large audience of trainees, the two trained prayer ministers moved to a private area and continued to pray with her. The prayer ministers told us later that Jesus did come into her memory and healed her deepest wounds.

The woman truly experienced freedom and understood God adopted her into His family and loved her unconditionally. He showed her she was not an accident in His eyes. She was a cherished daughter. With the assistance of the Holy Spirit and the trained prayer ministers, she forgave her mother and asked for forgiveness for agreements she made with the enemy about her self-worth.

When we understand we have agreed with the enemy, even if done inadvertently, we need to take the situation to the Lord for Him to heal. He will not erase the memory, but He will take the pain away. When we invite Him into a hurtful memory, He often has some loving thoughts, words, or images to share with us. First, we need to ask for forgiveness for any part we played in believing lies associated with the event. Then, we ask Him to fill us with blessings from the Holy Spirit.

Unforgiveness is another way the enemy gains a legal entrance to oppress us. Kail describes it as a perfect entry point. He saw many people freed from torment and physical illness when they forgave those who hurt and sinned against them.[6]

I grew up believing life was supposed to be fair, and I tried to make sure people treated me fairly. As a result, I did not want to let the people who hurt me off the hook easily. I erroneously believed the offender needed to demonstrate their remorse first—unaware this led to unforgiveness. The person who inflicted the pain hurt less than me.

Press and I witnessed tremendous healing in the people we prayed for when they forgave the individuals who hurt them. Their countenance changed in front of our eyes when we led them through prayers of forgiveness, and they accepted the Lord's forgiveness. They no longer sat with their heads and shoulders slumped over toward the floor. Their eyes sparkled with tears when they gazed up and smiled. Their exhilaration looked like they had burst out of the water after a jump off a diving board. They frequently told us they felt lighter, like a weight had lifted off them.

In 1 John 1:9 we are reminded we need to ask the Lord for His forgiveness. When we sincerely repent, He will forgive us.

The following sample prayer from our manual, *Simple Effective Prayer: A Model for Inner Healing,* can guide asking for forgiveness.

Pray aloud the bolded words:

> **Lord, You have made it clear that you want the healing and freedom for me that forgiveness brings. Therefore, I choose to forgive** *(name of person)* **for** *(what they did)* *(repeat as needed).* **I release _____ from any debt I believed was owed me. I repent for judging, and I let go of all judgments I had against _____ and any consequences or retributions I wanted for _____. I give all this over to You, Lord. I ask this in the name of Jesus.**

Chapter 3

Ancestral Influences

Negative ancestral influences, also referred to as generational curses, are another way the enemy can enter your family line. This is considered by many to be the biggest open door.

Kail defines a curse as "a supernatural force that brings harm or blocks the blessing of God."[7] My husband likes to describe negative ancestral influences by visualizing strings running through the family lines. If you consider yourself and your parents and their parents back to great-grandparents, you are looking at a minimum of thirty people connected by these invisible strings. Multiple marriages within families add more connections.

Negative spirits could have attached to any one of them and then passed down the family line. The odds none of these relatives made mistakes or did not make agreements with the lies of the enemy are slim. Almost all bloodlines have some destructive patterns that open doors.

Some prayer ministers refer to this as a generational curse or a negative ancestral influence. Our ancestors may have deliberately or unintentionally fallen into sin patterns, behaviors or habits, and attitudes that can influence us today. These generational influences do not necessarily make us sin, but they can cause us to lean to particular destructive patterns.

The concept of inherited tendencies is not new. Medical professionals are familiar with the idea of inheritance. They ask for a history of physical and mental illnesses in your relatives on initial patient interviews because they know these conditions can impact your current health.

Marilyn Hickey, minister and televangelist, describes the development of a generational curse as a process where a person practices a sin until it becomes a lifestyle. When the sin is entrenched, it becomes an iniquity or a bent toward a particular behavior. Repeated practice of the behavior allows the enemy to gain control in the family line.[8]

These negative influences can be repented of and broken so they no longer harm the person and their descendants. The key is recognizing and removing them.

Reaping the consequences of our ancestors' sins certainly seems unfair. We may not have known these relatives or have known what they did. We frequently heard prayer recipients tell us they felt drawn to certain activities (for example, alcohol, gambling, sexual sin, interest in the occult, fortune tellers, etc.), and they did not know why. When we ministered to them, the Lord showed them an open door in their bloodline.

Many people are unaware that we receive spiritual inheritances, both positive and negative, through our bloodlines. Some examples of negative ancestral influences or spirits include shame, fear, control, abandonment, anger, violence, abuse, addiction, sexual sin, and victimization. The appendix lists additional negative influences.

We need to understand these are negative spirits that have impacted people. They are not the person's identity. Awareness of these negative patterns provides information about where a possible door opened. We do not use this knowledge to blame our ancestors or others. Instead, we ask the Lord to close the door.

Prince suggested seven possible indications a curse may be operating in a family line. They are patterns of:

1. Mental or emotional breakdown
2. Repeated or chronic illness (especially if hereditary)
3. Barrenness, a tendency to miscarry or related female problems
4. Breakdown of marriage and family alienation
5. Continuing financial insufficiency
6. Being "accident-prone"
7. A family history of suicides or unnatural or untimely deaths[9]

During CHM's healing prayer training on generational curses, Press and I completed a family genogram depicting the negative influences and blessings we received from our relatives. The Holy Spirit revealed several female relatives on my father's side of the family who died young and under unusual or mysterious circumstances, suggesting a spirit of death operated in my family line. They died in their forties, and the oldest one died at age sixty-two.

When I received inner healing prayer several years later, the prayer minister asked me to talk about childhood dreams. I had not thought about childhood dreams for decades. The Holy Spirit immediately brought to mind my fear of death around the age of eleven. I was concerned I might die in a car accident, and this fear lingered for almost a year.

On my way to school one morning at age eleven, a car nearly hit me when it drove over the curb and into the middle of a front lawn where I stood waiting for my friends. I was not physically hurt, just shook up. It certainly was a bizarre situation, and I never found out why the car drove off the road onto the middle of the lawn and then quickly drove away.

Six months before I turned sixty-two, I received the diagnosis of follicular lymphoma, a blood cancer. My oncologist said this type of cancer was not curable, but treatable and it would return. Several months later, a visiting pastor came to our church to teach about healing. When he finished, he said he wanted to pray individually for those who needed a physical touch from the Lord. When I told him that I had been diagnosed with follicular lymphoma, he asked me what traumatic event occurred in my life in the previous six months. I surprised myself when I responded that my brother died from leukemia six months earlier. I had not connected my brother's death to my illness. I also heard other healing prayer ministers say that cancer manifests in a person after a traumatic event.

I do not know how—or when—the spirit of death first entered my family line, but it certainly wreaked havoc throughout the generations. I learned that several other family members experienced near-death events. We were not aware there might be a connection to negative ancestral influences or generational curses at the time of these frightening episodes. The Bible tells us the enemy seeks to destroy us. I believe he is happy when we remain ignorant of the supernatural occurrences in our midst and of the power and authority we have in Jesus to fight and remove them.

The good news is we can take authority over these negative influences, as Jesus tells us in Luke 10:19. When we acknowledge destructive patterns exist in our ancestry and ask for forgiveness, we affirm we want it to stop right now and not impact our future generations. We choose blessings over curses, and these blessings extend into eternity. We are not casting blame on our ancestors.

Hickey and her daughter, Sarah Bowling, remind us that no family member, whether alive or dead, truly makes us sin because we have the freedom to choose our actions. They also assert that it only takes one individual in a family to turn things around and break the negative patterns.[10]

I broke the spirit of death off my life and the lives of my family members with the help of the prayer minister who asked me about my childhood dreams. She clarified this was a generational curse, and as Christians, we possess the power and authority to break this influence off our lives. Then she guided me to say a prayer similar to the one Press and I later developed for the SEP manual.

The following sample prayer from *Simple Effective Prayer: A Model for Inner Healing* can guide breaking negative ancestral influences.

Pray aloud the bolded words:

1. **I confess the sins of my ancestors, my parents, and my sins associated with** *(the negative ancestral influence)*, **and I forgive**

each person for how these influences have hurt me *(Under the guidance of the Holy Spirit, name the people aloud).* I choose to forgive _____, _____, _____, _____.

2.   Lord, I ask You to forgive me for yielding to these negative influences. I receive Your forgiveness, and I choose to forgive myself for entering into these sins.

3.   I renounce these negative influences and break their power over my life, my family, and all future family in Jesus's holy name.

4.   I receive God's blessings and replace *(the negative ancestral influence)* with _____, _____, _____ *(Ask the Holy Spirit what He wants to fill you with to replace what was renounced).*

CHAPTER 4

Word Curses

Word curses are another type of curse or negative influence. Some comments include:

"You will never amount to anything."

"If people really knew you, no one would want you."

"You are a failure."

"You are so dumb."

"I am stupid."

"I can never do anything right."

These are hurtful words spoken over us. Others can say word curses over us, or we can repeat them over ourselves. The critical point here is the person accepted them as valid, which led them to believe lies about themselves.

Proverbs 18:21 warns us "death and life are in the power of the tongue." James 3:10 tells us, "From the same mouth come blessing and cursing. My brothers, these things ought not to be so." Our words carry power. We must carefully choose them when we speak to others and talk about ourselves.

People in authority can speak negative words over others purposely or unintentionally. Bernie Siegel, M.D., recounts numerous stories of people with terminal illnesses whose physicians told them that they did not have long to live or the doctors could do no more. Unfortunately, some people received this as a pronouncement of their death, and they did die soon after hearing these words.

Others chose to pray and have a positive attitude, and they lived and did not die as their doctors predicted. Siegel believes their positive attitude and beliefs made a difference in their outcome. He proposes how we think and feel affects our health because our minds and bodies are connected. He comments that refusing to hope is, in essence, a decision to die.[11]

My oncologist reminded me several times that follicular lymphoma is not curable and would reoccur. She added that many patients continue to lead long lives while working with their physicians to manage the disease. She did not make a pronouncement of death over me. If I chose to focus on the words "it is not curable," I could have received her news as a word curse.

I understand existing research data indicate this type of cancer is not currently curable with available interventions. I am also careful not to receive the statement regarding this condition as incurable as a proclamation that this is the only outcome possible. I do not want to live my life by making this a self-fulfilling prophecy.

Sometimes negative words are spoken over unborn children while they are in their mother's womb. Over the past several decades, we have become more aware of the importance of prenatal life. We are certainly mindful of the significance of the pregnant mother's nutrition on her unborn child's physical health. We may not be aware of the spiritual and emotional factors during this critical period in the unborn child's life. CHM has an excellent teaching on conception to birth prayers. These prayers invite Jesus into the memory from conception to birth to ask Him when trauma or unkind words may have occurred during this time.[12]

We also are aware the environment and parents' attitudes about pregnancy can impact the growing fetus. If a baby was unwanted or rejected while in the womb, or turmoil or violence occurred in the family's home, the child might carry some anxiety into adulthood.

During the writing of this book, Press and I prayed with a young woman, Sarah, who learned that her anxiety began in the womb when her mother got pregnant before her wedding date. The fact her mother got pregnant before she married was never openly discussed with Sarah by her parents. Although Sarah felt loved by both parents, she still experienced anxiety throughout her life. She previously believed the root of her anxiety concerned a challenging childhood relationship. During the prayer session, the Lord showed her this nervousness began before her birth. Sarah acknowledged she sensed her mother's tension while in the womb. She then understood a spirit of anxiety had been prevalent in her family line for several generations, and negative words may have been spoken. Sarah prayed to break off the spirit of anxiety using the prayer to break negative ancestral influences.

If the child was not the gender the parents desired, a spirit of rejection might take hold. I felt loved by my parents, and they verbally told me they loved me. In my early adult years, I learned that my parents hoped their first-born child would be a boy. At the time of my birth, there were no sonograms available to show the baby's gender, so parents did not know if they were having a boy or girl until the birth. I was the first grandchild born on both sides of my family.

In my forties, my aunt gave me the letter she wrote to her parents on my birthday. The opening line read, *"It's the most beautiful baby I've ever seen."* My aunt and my father cried with relief when they saw that I appeared healthy after the lengthy and challenging delivery. When my mother awoke from the sedation, my aunt asked what she thought of her new daughter. My mother said I looked like my grandfather, so he would not mind that I was a girl. Then my aunt wrote, "A grandson next time, maybe." My grandfather had two daughters and no sons, which he desired. Fortunately, I did feel genuinely cherished by my aunts, uncles, and grandparents during my childhood.

For sixty years, my mother openly acknowledged being partial to boys, particularly my two younger brothers. For most of my married life, I lived 700 miles away from my mother. My brothers lived seven miles from her in her later years. I made a last-minute decision to join my family for a brief visit one afternoon in 2013, just after I attended a CHM training three hours from my brother's home. I beckoned my mother several times to come and sit with me in my brother's living room, knowing I could only spend a few hours with the family before I needed to return home to work the following day. Everyone knew this needed to be a short visit. Instead, my mother chose to remain in the kitchen with my brothers, who lived in the same town.

In my mind, I replayed the events of the short visit while we drove home that evening. My heart ached and my eyes burned with tears as feelings of rejection and sadness surfaced. I could not fathom why my mother would not join me in the living room so we could spend time together. I called her while Press drove and asked if she was mad at me or if I had offended her. She insisted she was not mad at me, and I had not upset her. She said she just felt comfortable with my brothers and did not want to intrude on my conversation with my sister-in-law and niece.

She reminded me boys were "still a novelty" because there weren't many boys in her family. When she used the word "novelty" again about my brothers, I felt like a knife pierced my heart. The newness had not worn off after sixty years. This comment also triggered memories from my growing-up years when I heard relatives say it was best to have a son as your first-born child. I had buried these memories, but they resurfaced when I heard, "boys are a novelty." The family passed down this belief for several generations. Afterward, I needed to forgive my mother for this perceived rejection and receive more healing from the Lord.

We must be careful with our spoken words. They can have a powerful impact and cause intense wounding. Words may have been spoken over children by well-meaning parents trying to shape their children's behavior in the way they learned from their parents. A child may have heard, "You are obnoxious just like your Aunt Doris!" or "You are just like your Uncle Sid, who never amounted to anything." The parents' intent may have been to warn the child their behavior was not acceptable and needed to change. The child could, however, interpret these comments as reflective of their true identity, causing them to believe they could not change. The issue here is we carry our wounding until we receive healing.

If our parents were wounded emotionally and were criticized and heard harsh words from their parents, they may continue this pattern with their children. In my work as a counselor and psychologist, I often heard parents say the beatings and screaming arguments they endured from their parents were not a problem as they enthusiastically announced, "After all, I turned out okay." Yes, they did survive and often became good citizens. Nevertheless, deep wounds remained that were never dealt with and were left unresolved.

The following sample prayer from our manual, *Simple Effective Prayer: A Model for Inner Healing,* can guide breaking word curses.

Pray aloud the bolded words:

1. **I forgive** (could be myself) _____ **for cursing me by saying, "**_____.**"**

2. **I repent for receiving this word curse and allowing it to influence my thoughts and behavior. Lord, I ask You to forgive me, and I receive Your forgiveness.**

3. **I renounce and break all agreements with this word curse, and I cancel all resulting judgments based on Jesus's sacrifice on the cross.**

   At this point, have the person pause and ask the Lord for His truth.

4. **The truth is** _____.

CHAPTER 5

The Occult

Any involvement with the occult can give access to negative influences. Reese and Barnett, inner healing ministers and authors of *Freedom Tools*, suggest many reasons people turn to the occult, including a desire for protection, power, or a yearning for supernatural knowledge.[13] Occult practices could include reading horoscopes, visiting fortune tellers, séances, playing with a Ouija board, and using Tarot cards, to name a few. Reese and Barnett state that even though many of these practices may seem respectable, they all stem from witchcraft. They refer to witchcraft as demonic manipulation used for control and domination.[14]

Individuals involved in occult practices have cast spells or curses over others to seek revenge or manipulate. Although this practice may seem far-fetched in our western culture, it does happen. As a young adult, I was surprised to learn that my friend Jake's mother believed in occult practices. She cast spells on others, including her children. These spells and curses continued to impact Jake and his sister negatively in adulthood.

When I grew up in the Sixties, a popular Christmas gift was a Ouija Board, also known as talking board or spirit board. This game included a board marked with letters of the alphabet, numbers, and the words "yes," "no," and "good-bye." Participants asked questions and placed their fingers on a plastic or wooden object that moved around the board to spell out the answers. My parents bought this game for my brother and me as a joint Christmas gift.

Playing with the Ouija Board seemed like innocent fun at that time, and no one recognized that this naïve curiosity could open the door to darkness. Fortunately, my brother and I only used the Ouija Board a couple of times. Later, as an adult, when I learned this could open the door to negative spirits, I renounced it and asked the Lord for forgiveness and requested Jesus to close this door. I felt a sense of peace afterward.

In my teens, my friends and I read our horoscopes for fun. Again, we had no idea this practice was not wise. The horoscopes in the newspaper naturally piqued our interest in learning each day's prediction. As with the Ouija Board, I later renounced this.

Each of these practices seeks information about the future through means other than asking the Lord. The enemy loves to take advantage of this and have you seek power and authority through him rather than through God. Remember, the devil tried to coerce Jesus into following him by promising Him all the kingdoms of the world. (See Matthew Chapter 4.) As believers in Jesus, we have higher power and authority in our Lord. We need to recognize this power and authority and exercise it by leaning into Him for direction in all areas of our lives.

Involvement in false belief systems, cults, and secret societies, are other avenues the enemy uses to access a person's life.

New Age teachings are an example of a false belief system based on partial truths. These teachings can be compelling because they often use Christian terms and refer to Jesus. They do not describe the same Jesus portrayed in the Bible. Jesus is referred to as an esteemed spiritual teacher, but not as the Son of God. Some New Age teachings promote the belief we are all gods and can become one with the universe through self-spirituality. Some teachings claim we have forgotten our own divinity.

The deception comes when they emphasize the person's spiritual authority comes from within the individual. Christians believe their power and authority are based on the finished work of Jesus Christ on the cross. Thus, a Christian's identity is rooted in Christ, not in the belief of their own divinity.

Many cults have deceived and misled people throughout history. Their charismatic leaders use false teachings and manipulation to control and exploit their followers and their doctrines do not line up with the character of God.

Reverend Jim Jones founded the Peoples Temple in Indiana in the mid-1950s. He later moved to California and then to Guyana. His passion for civil rights appealed to those who followed him. After a Congressional visit, he panicked and ordered his followers to drink cyanide-laced grape punch to commit suicide in Jonestown, Guyana, in 1978. More than 900 followers died. Other well-known cult groups include the Branch Davidians led by David Koresh and Heaven's Gate led by Marshall Applewhite.

Involvement in secret societies is another way darkness can enter a person's life, and members can come under the authority of false teaching. These organizations and associations have appealed to people who found their identity and connection with others through membership in these exclusive groups.

One well-known organization active today that requires initiation rituals and has its members swear to secrecy is the Freemasons. Robert L. D. Cooper, Curator of the Scottish Masonic Museum Library at the Freemason's Hall in Edinburgh, said men are attracted to the organization for the following reasons: companionship and enjoyment in their social activities, admiration of others who were Masons, family associations, the possibility of doing good and helping others, the esoteric aspects of the organization, and the opportunity for rituals and role-playing.[15] We have known individuals who claimed they only received business contracts because they were Masons. Former Masons have written about Freemasonry's deception that begins when the candidate is initiated and continues throughout all degrees attained.

Jack Harris, a former leader (Worshipful Master) of a Masonic lodge, writes that the organization deceives unsuspecting people of its pagan rituals, including church leaders, by using some biblical terminology in its rights and initiations. He said Freemasonry believes a person's character and good deeds determine their destiny rather than the finished work of Christ on the cross. Harris asserts that the organization wants its candidates to speak only with other Masons when seeking truths.[16]

John Salza, another former Mason, describes the rituals and the deception in recruitment, initiation, and covenant oaths in *Masonry Unmasked: An Insider Reveals the Secrets of the Lodge.* He writes that Masons swear to secrecy regarding their doctrines and practices and bind themselves and their families to severe penalties if they break their oaths. These covenant oaths and the hidden meaning of the rituals remain undisclosed in advance to the candidate seeking to be a Freemason.[17]

Salza states many Masons are moral and righteous people. Some Christians who remain in the organization do not regularly attend meetings and are unaware of the rituals and their meanings. Other Christians stay in the Lodge even after acknowledging the contradiction between their faith and the Freemasons' teachings because they rationalize the positives outweigh the negatives. After all, the Masons participate in charitable activities for their communities, and the Lodge provides a support system for them, especially when they experience hardships. They question why other Christians criticize their organization when they do so much good.[18]

My husband and I have prayed to break curses associated with Freemasonry with people whose parents or ancestors were Freemasons. They suffered as a result of covenants and agreements their ancestors made years before, which manifested in their current lives in physical ailments, as well as intense fear. Some people did not personally know their ancestor, who was a Freemason. In the prayer session, they renounced the oaths and curses associated with the various degrees of Freemasonry.

Contact with unholy things, including various types of media and objects, can allow darkness an opening to operate in your life. Exposure to pornography, horror movies, and violence can invite spirits of fear, lust, or aggression.

Prince described how he first became aware of the curses unholy objects can bring. His grandfather brought home four beautifully embroidered imperial dragons from the Boxer Rebellion in China, and Prince inherited them after his grandfather's death. Prince hung these artwork pieces in his home because they brought back memories of his time as a child in his grandfather's house. Around the time he hung them in his house, he noticed opposition in his ministry. He prayed over the situation and sensed the dragon represented Satan. Prince got rid of the artwork, which he believed brought a curse into his house, and experienced God's blessings almost immediately—improvement in his finances when his income more than doubled and a delayed inheritance from his mother's estate.[19]

My family may have unknowingly been exposed to unholy objects when my brother brought home souvenirs from his overseas naval career travels. One time, he gave our mother a set of shields and some other items from a trip to Africa. My mother hung them on the wall in her family room. We were unaware of the impact of evil forces at that time.

Many years later, when my mother removed the shields and other souvenirs, she said she noticed a definite peace in her home that had been absent for some time. She asked me if I thought the presence of the shields had caused the perceived tension. Although not all items from Africa may have had occult attachments, my mother's souvenir shields may have carried some negative influences.

When we are aware of occult influences in our lives, we can reject and renounce them and ask for forgiveness for any part we may have played in holding on to these effects. If a generational pattern is identified, we can use the prayer suggested under negative ancestral influences.

Pray aloud the following bolded words from the SEP manual that my husband and I wrote:

> **I completely sever all contact with the occult, and I break the power of** *(Name the specific form(s) of the occult here)* **over my life and the lives of my current family and future generations, based on the finished work of Christ on the cross.**

The person needs to ask for blessings from the Holy Spirit in place of these negative occult influences and request an infilling of the Lord's truth and peace.

CHAPTER 6

Soul Ties

Unhealthy or ungodly soul ties are another access point for darkness. Soul ties are unseen spiritual bonds formed when we are in a close relationship with someone, such as a family member, close friend, boss, or person in authority. Bill and Sue Banks, authors of *Breaking Unhealthy Soul-ties*, describe a soul tie as a joining together of two souls that become as one.[20]

God ordained marriage as a covenant agreement between two individuals of the opposite sex to bond and become one. Soul ties develop when we are in a sexual relationship. These connections were intended to be godly soul ties experienced within the covenant of marriage. God at the center of this marriage bond forms a healthy soul tie. God designed us to be in a relationship with Him and with each other. Our first and essential soul tie is union with Jesus.

Sometimes our relationships with other people can become unhealthy, and this can open the door for sin to enter our lives and put us in bondage and turmoil, which binds us in spiritual chains. We refer to this as an unhealthy or ungodly soul tie.

Unhealthy soul ties develop when we are in a sexual relationship outside of marriage. Controlling and manipulative relationships also form unhealthy bonds and provide the environment for the enemy to negatively impact people. Over-dependence on another person may indicate an unhealthy soul tie is operating. Young children need to be dependent on their parents for guidance and protection. Except for young children who need to rely on their parents, no one should control another person.

David Cross, author of *Soul Ties: The Unseen Bond in Relationships,* indicates that Freemasonry's rituals represent powerful and ungodly control over the members' lives that progressively tie them to other members and the organization's spiritual and physical authorities.[21] When someone is afraid of another person, this may indicate an unhealthy soul tie. The Banks note that people who try to control others are often motivated by fear, such as a fear of rejection. This fear can be rooted in abandonment experienced at a young age. They indicate that unhealthy soul ties typically develop over time and can be subtle and grow like cancer.[22]

The following scenario from our manual, *Simple Effective Prayer: A Model for Inner Healing,* illustrates an unhealthy soul tie based on control and manipulation between Mary and her adult daughter, Sandy:

Mary, an elderly mother, has enough money to live independently in a lovely retirement community, and she is in good health. Accustomed to manipulating others to get what she wants, she tries to convince her adult daughter, Sandy, that she must live with her instead of moving to a retirement community. Sandy has a full-time job, and she and her husband are raising three daughters. Despite being active in her community and church, Sandy makes time to visit her mother regularly and phone and check on her. Lately, Mary's demands have become intolerable, and Sandy can never seem to do enough to satisfy her mother's desires. Mary tells Sandy, "Remember all that I have done for you," "What will others think if you don't let me move in with you?", "After all, I may not live much longer," and "It is your responsibility to care for me." As a result, Sandy experiences guilt and condemnation, resulting from the unhealthy soul tie.

Just as Sandy did not realize unhealthy soul ties existed, many people are unaware of their presence and the negative impact on their lives. Kris Vallotton of Bethel Church notes the following seven ways that can reveal if you have an unhealthy soul tie with someone:

1. You are in an abusive relationship (physically, emotionally, or spiritually), but you feel so close to the person that you refuse to set boundaries or cut off the connection.

2. You cannot get the person out of your mind even though you may have left the relationship a long time ago.

3. You feel as if the person is with you or watching you whenever you do anything.

4. You still visualize the person you have a soul tie with when you are in an intimate relationship with someone else.

5. You take on the negative characteristics of that person and carry their offenses even if you disagree with them.

6. You defend your right to remain in an unhealthy relationship even though the relationship adversely affects you or destroys other significant relationships in your life.

7. You notice simultaneous experiences or moods as the person you have a soul tie with, including sickness, accidents, and addictions.[23]

It is important to note several other vital points associated with soul ties. First, relationships can have a mixture of good and bad soul ties. You can break the unhealthy connection while maintaining or strengthening the healthy soul tie. Second, because soul ties are established in the spirit realm, they are not limited by time and place. We can have a soul tie with a dead person.

John 11:25 quotes Jesus as saying, "I am the resurrection and the life. Whoever believes in me, though he die, yet shall he live." Although we separate from our physical bodies at the time of death, our spirits still exist. Feeling plagued with negative thoughts or excessively bound to a deceased person can signal the presence of an unhealthy soul tie. The Banks couple assert soul ties involving sexual contact and those rooted in the occult seem to be the strongest and most challenging to break.[24] Some side effects of unhealthy soul ties include:

- Loss of independence and self-confidence
- Loss of clear thinking when making decisions
- Loss of peace
- Loss of the capability to rightly love others
- Loss of spiritual liberation and personal freedom
- Loss of good health accompanied by illness
- Loss of closeness to Father God[25]

Jesus can break unhealthy soul ties. First, we must be aware they are operating and ask the Lord for His mercy and grace to break them. Next, we need to confess our part in the unhealthy soul tie, forgive those who have wounded us, and then by faith, receive God's freedom in breaking the unseen, unhealthy bond. The essential soul tie for Christians must be with Jesus Christ. He brings restoration and peace.

Our friend Nita related a poignant story about the impact of a soul tie in her life. Nita and her current husband, Jim, are healing prayer ministers. They have guided many people in breaking unhealthy soul ties, and they broke unhealthy soul ties in their lives as well. Before marrying Jim, Nita was in a challenging marriage for more than twenty-five years with a man who dealt with multiple mental health issues. Nita believed she had broken the unhealthy soul ties with her former husband many years earlier.

Nearly twenty-five years after their divorce, Nita experienced severe headaches and pain that required medical treatment. Unfortunately, the pain did not dissipate with treatment. At this same time, Nita's former husband was ill and near death and asked her to pray with him. Jim, Nita, and her two daughters from that marriage went to her ex's home to pray. Despite breaking soul ties in the past, Nita felt the Lord's leading that evening to pray to cut each person there free from any remaining unhealthy connections.

Shortly after their prayer time, the ex-husband's wife called and informed Nita that her ex had passed away. Nita also noticed that after weeks of suffering, her pain and headaches were immediately gone after the family cut themselves free from any negative attachments during that prayer time.

While I listened to Nita's story, I noted the importance of following the Lord's leading. Nita prayed to cut herself and the others free, despite believing she previously dealt with unhealthy ties. Spiritual connections, both healthy and unhealthy, can be strong and influential despite being unseen. As a result of following the Lord's leading, Nita received incredible physical and spiritual healing.

The following sample prayer from our manual, *Simple Effective Prayer: A Model for Inner Healing,* can guide breaking unhealthy soul ties.

Pray aloud the bolded words:

1. **By the power of Jesus's holy name and His shed blood on the cross, I confess all unhealthy soul ties with _____.**

2. **I forgive _____ for their part in this unhealthy soul tie and all the ways it has affected my family and me.**

3. **I ask Your forgiveness Lord for any part I played in this unhealthy soul tie.**

4. **I give back to _____ everything that I may have taken from _____, and I take back everything _____ took from me, including from my heart.**

5. **I renounce and break this unhealthy soul tie with _____, and I release myself from_____. I am free. I renounce and cancel any darkness associated with this soul tie. I am completely restored, and I pray _____ is completely restored.**

6. **I pray blessings on _____.**

SECTION 3

Forgiveness

Many people do not understand forgiveness and how to apply it. Forgiveness is essential for your freedom and is not an option. You need to ask the Lord to show you any areas of unforgiveness in your life. Then forgive those who offended you. You may need to forgive yourself and release anger toward God. If you cannot forgive, ask the Lord to help you. He can handle your anger and will not reject you. He loves you regardless of your feelings for Him.

CHAPTER 7

Understanding Forgiveness

In my fifties, I finally learned the importance of forgiveness and why withholding it is not an option for Christians. For years, I erroneously believed I needed to hold out for fairness to be rendered first or for the offender to show remorse before I forgave them. I thought they needed to earn their forgiveness. By not forgiving, I partnered with the enemy by believing these lies, and consequently, I allowed him to wreak havoc in my life.

The enemy only has the authority we give him. We provide him with power when we agree with him by believing his lies, knowingly or unknowingly. I failed to understand that my role did not include acting as the judge and jury of my offender. God is the only judge who will execute justice.

Forgiving people who hurt us brings us freedom. When we do not forgive them, they still have power over us until we release them. The person who won't forgive becomes the victim. Rodney Hogue, pastor and author of *Forgiveness*, writes this is similar to putting poison in a cup for the offender, hoping to punish him, and then drinking it yourself.[1]

The medical profession says we make ourselves physically ill when we refuse to forgive and hold onto anger. Chronic anger affects our heart rate, blood pressure, and immune response, putting us at risk for conditions such as heart disease, depression, and diabetes. Forgiving others provides benefits such as improved cholesterol levels and sleep, a lowered risk of heart attack, and a reduction in pain, blood pressure, and levels of anxiety, depression, and stress.[2]

Bitterness

When we do not forgive our offenders and cut them free, bitterness can enter our hearts. Bitterness is a stronghold or an entrenched thought pattern that can occur when we hold onto unmet expectations. When we remain bitter, we mistakenly think those who hurt us suffer punishment as long as we hold on to revenge. We then believe the lie that it is up to us to keep the offense alive.

God is the only one who vindicates. In Deuteronomy 32:35, God tells his people "Vengeance is mine." This phrase repeats in the New Testament in Romans 12:19, which states, "Beloved, never avenge yourselves, but leave it to the wrath of God, for it is written, 'Vengeance is mine, I will repay, says the Lord.'"

Giving up our bitterness and unforgiveness allows the Holy Spirit to work in our lives and fill us with peace and joy. Unfortunately, the enemy wants to use unforgiveness to steal and destroy our destiny.

Extending forgiveness can be one of the most challenging things we need to do, especially when mistreated. My husband and I facilitated healing prayer training in our home several years ago. One of our friends invited a woman she worked with to join the group training that evening as a guest. No one, including us, had met this woman before. The deep lines in her face, her piercing eyes, and her hypervigilant stance suggested a life filled with severe challenges and bitterness.

The woman was unaware of the topic for the evening. The Lord knew the teaching focus, and most likely, this was a divine appointment for her.

Judith MacNutt's DVD teaching focused on forgiveness that evening. She indicated the majority of Jesus's teachings directly related to forgiveness and love. She emphasized the value of listening to the prayer recipient's story before we pray. Listening is vital because many people do not have someone to share their pain with, so they internalize their hurtful experiences. These broken and unforgiven parts of their life become toxic until they are brought to Jesus to shed His light on and bring transformation and healing.

MacNutt also explained the importance of listening to the Holy Spirit when we pray with others because only He can convict people of sin and comes with mercy and grace to bring freedom. She related stories of people she witnessed forgiving those who previously inflicted horrific hurt and pain on them. She suggested we view the prayer recipient's pain as a gift that reveals the source of the wounds in need of healing. The emotions attached to the offense frequently have been buried alive and need to be given to Jesus to remove the pain and heal the person. She emphasized God's timing is critical in the process of forgiveness, and the person needs to be ready to decide to do this.

We continued to watch the DVD training while MacNutt modeled the forgiveness principles. She concluded by sharing that sometimes a person may say they will never forgive another person. This refusal comes from a deep well of hurt. The Bible indicates we are to forgive *all* who sin against us, not just a few. We also are to pray for our enemies. Jesus said in Luke 6:27–28, "But I say to you who hear, Love your enemies, do good to those who hate you, bless those who curse you, pray for those who abuse you." It is God's love in us that extends this love to our enemy. We do not do this on our own or out of our strength.

After watching the DVD, our friend asked if we could pray for her guest. The guest agreed she would like to receive prayer, so we gathered around her to pray. Before we prayed, she yelled that her brother raped her at age sixteen, and her mother forced her to have an abortion. "He should rot in hell for what he did to me," the guest said. "I will never forgive him for what he did. He does not deserve my forgiveness." Her outburst continued when she said her brother had died and repeated he should burn in hell.

No one argued with her or tried to persuade her to forgive her brother at that moment. She was not ready to forgive him or her mother. While we processed the teaching we had watched together and shared refreshments, we continued to interact with our guest in a kind and non-judgmental manner, similar to how MacNutt demonstrated. After the woman left, we agreed to individually pray throughout the following week for the Lord to minister to her. If she could allow the Holy Spirit to help her forgive, she could receive freedom from the pain and hurt she endured for over thirty-five years.

So, What is Forgiveness?

Kendall asserts forgiveness is practiced daily and is a life-long commitment. He reminds us the Lord's Prayer demonstrates we need daily forgiveness as much as we require daily bread.[3] We need to pray each day for the grace to forgive others. When we harbor unforgiveness, it blocks our intimate relationship with the Lord. The enemy loves to see us disconnected from God. Kendall emphasizes our inability to forgive is the single greatest weakness Satan loves to exploit.[4]

Many people misunderstand the concept of forgiveness. Clarification regarding forgiveness follows in the table below:

Forgiveness is NOT:	Forgiveness is:
forgetting what happened or erasing a memory	releasing the power the memory has over you
saying what the offender did was okay	acknowledging the wrongdoing but choosing to let it go
a feeling	a choice, a decision, or an act of the will
saying there is no debt owed	canceling that debt
saying reconciliation of the relationship is the next step	necessary, but reconciliation is not necessary
releasing your boundaries and saying anything goes	recognizing it may be unsafe to be around the offenders even though you forgave them
letting the person off the hook	transferring the person to Jesus's hook
dependent on the actions and choices of the offender	dependent on your choice to forgive regardless of the offender's response
done to benefit the offender	done to benefit the person who was offended or hurt

One common misconception regarding forgiveness is that you will forget what the offender did to you or erase the memory from your mind. We have heard people question whether they have forgiven someone because they still remember what happened to them. You will still recall the event. When you forgive, you release the power the situation and offender have over you. You give the pain associated with the offense to Jesus to heal. We are not supposed to do this on our own. Hogue refers to this as "transferring that person from 'your hook' to 'Jesus's hook.'"[5]

When you transfer the wrongdoer to Jesus's hook, you relinquish your right to enforce justice and turn the person over to the Lord. If you decide not to free that individual, you show you want to stand in God's place as the judge and take revenge. This decision is not a good plan. The Lord warns us regarding the seriousness of judging others.

In Matthew 7:1–2, Jesus said, "Judge not, that you be not judged. For with the judgment you pronounce you will be judged, and with the measure you use it will be measured to you."

Press and I have prayed with men in the prison who told us they could not rest until they sought revenge for violence against them. They did not understand that their judgment and unforgiveness robbed them of the freedom they desired.

One twenty-three-year-old man we encountered, Alexander, described the anger that boiled inside while he plotted ways to inflict bodily harm on the people who hurt him and his family. Nightmares filled with rage and murderous plans interrupted his attempts to sleep at night. Waking moments were preoccupied with thoughts of revenge and plans to trap the men who physically had harmed him. He wanted his perpetrators to suffer and fear for their lives, as he did when attacked. Alexander's attempt to enact justice on his perpetrators resulted in his arrest. He did not experience the emotional release or peace he imagined would follow after he hurt the men who wounded him. He suffered from headaches, nightmares, and physical exhaustion while incarcerated.

Alexander requested a prayer appointment because he wanted the Lord to heal his angry heart and give him peace. Press and I shared the importance of forgiveness for his freedom. We clarified that forgiveness did not mean the harm he experienced was okay. He was mistreated and did not deserve the beatings. Alexander wanted release from the memory of the violent attack. When he understood that the only way to experience peace was to hand the perpetrators over to Jesus, he extended his hands upward and asked Jesus to take this burden. He relinquished the role of judge to the Lord.

Alexander asked us to guide him in a prayer to forgive the men who hurt him. His jaw relaxed, his clenched fists opened, and he looked serenely happy after he forgave the men. He told us he believed the Lord blanketed him in peace after he prayed.

When we invite Jesus into the painful memory during inner healing prayer, He often shows us where He was at that time, and He takes the heartache away when we give it to Him. The key is we need to give our hurts to Him, as Alexander did. When Jesus heals, He frequently shows the person some aspect of the painful situation they were not aware of when it occurred. Jesus can do this because He transcends time and space.

Toward the end of the prayer session, Alexander sat back in his chair, put his hand on his forehead, and shook his head from side to side. Press and I asked him what was happening. Alexander said he sensed for the first time that Jesus had prevented a fatal attack. Unbeknownst to him at the time of the attack, Jesus was there and saved his life.

You must recognize forgiveness is not excusing, pardoning, or justifying what the person did. You are not negating the seriousness of what happened to you. You are acknowledging the wrongdoing but choosing to let it go. The person does owe you a debt, but you decide not to demand it from them. You choose to cancel it by turning the person and situation over to Jesus for Him to deal with them, as Alexander did. Most likely, the person does not deserve your forgiveness. Our Lord has forgiven us of much, and we do not deserve it. David writes in Psalm 103 that God removes our sins "as far as the east is from the west."

The Lord is calling us to be compassionate and merciful. Forgiving is not asking you to pretend or deny the wrongdoing happened or it did not hurt. We may feel bitter because of our expectations in the situation. Press and

I prayed with people who sobbed while they described their relationships with their parents. Some said their parents did not love them. Others said their parents rejected them. We guided them in prayer to give their unmet expectations regarding their parents to the Lord and ask for His help to forgive them. Several people told us they sensed the Lord lifted a weight off their shoulders when they forgave their parents. Others said they were no longer locked in resentment. Sometimes the Lord showed them a picture of their parents as wounded individuals. They then understood their parents were not able to love them the way they desired.

In my late twenties, I forgave my parents for not meeting some of my needs. My parents said they were sorry for any emotional pain I experienced as a result of their parenting. My mother admitted that she was unaware that I had needs. My parents' willingness to engage in conversations I initiated about my childhood strengthened our relationship. I thought their acknowledgment of my hurt would bring the complete relief I sought. It did not. I remained baffled by occasional feelings of disappointment.

After completing a Master's degree in counseling at age thirty-one, I sought help to understand my frustration. I had forgiven my parents, but I could not fathom why they had not pursued help to deal with their woundedness. If they had received counseling support, perhaps they would have been emotionally available to meet their children's needs. I thought this might have alleviated my suffering. I tried not to focus on my unmet expectations, but these thoughts would periodically resurface. I could not figure out how to let go of the disappointment and remained stuck clinging to my expectations.

Almost twenty years later, I learned through healing prayer that I also needed to release my unmet expectations and disappointment to the Lord. I did this through prayer and daily conversations with the Lord. Several years later, a friend encouraged me to journal my feelings to the Lord and listen for His response. His reply often came as a thought, picture in my mind, or a memory. The Lord reminded me there are no perfect parents. Sometimes our parents cannot give us the emotional support we need because of their wounding or lack of modeling from their parents. I also learned the Lord meets all our needs when we ask Him. He can fill in the gaps where our parents were not emotionally available.

Another common misconception concerning forgiveness relates to boundaries. Forgiveness does not mean you release your boundaries and allow the person to do whatever they want. If abuse has occurred, it may not be safe to be around this person again after you have forgiven them. It would be best if you established safe physical and emotional boundaries. The court system may need to deal with the situation, and the guilty party may face punishment under the law. By forgiving the offender, you are cutting yourself free from the power the person and situation have over you, so bitterness does not reign in your heart. If you choose not to forgive, you are attaching yourself to the offense and that person.

We cannot wait to forgive until we feel like forgiving. Forgiving is a conscious decision of the will. It is not a feeling. Frequently, we do not feel like absolving the person. We do it as an act of obedience to the Lord, and we trust the emotions will follow later. Waiting until you feel like forgiving is not the best gauge of whether or not you should forgive. We can remain locked in bitterness if we do not forgive. Bitterness robs us of peace and joy and can manifest in physical ailments.

Even after we have forgiven someone, we may begin to experience feelings of unforgiveness. We are not to let this derail us. As we allow the Lord to transform our minds, the emotions and feelings of forgiveness will follow. The Lord healed my emotions regarding my unmet expectations when I finally released them.

In many instances, the person who harmed you may never know you forgave them. Forgiveness benefits us, not the guilty party. It opens the door to the love and joy the Lord has for us and is the key to our freedom. Forgiveness is not dependent on the transgressor's actions and choices but rather on the will of the injured person to forgive, regardless of the offender's response.

Forgiving someone does not require reconciliation. Although we may want to resolve issues with the wrongdoer, we need to realize that our relationship with them is not necessarily the next step. Perhaps the offender does not wish to reconcile. They may not be ready or at a place to rebuild the relationship, or they may not be repentant or remorseful. If that individual is dangerous or abusive, reconciliation is probably not wise. In any case, we are required to forgive.

Reconciliation depends on the offender's willingness to discuss the situation and involves the cooperation of both that person and the individual hurt. Forgiveness depends only on the person wounded. We need to keep in mind that although reconciliation is preferred and undoubtedly an added benefit, our first objective is to set things straight with God and get free of the bondage of bitterness. If the Lord leads us to seek further restoration, we must obey Him.

Pray this prayer aloud:

> Now that I have a clearer understanding of forgiveness, I relinquish my offender to You, Lord, as the only judge and jury. I no longer want to be a victim and give power to my offender or the enemy. I ask for Your forgiveness for trying to enforce justice and holding on to false beliefs about forgiveness. Lord, I want to hear clearly from the Holy Spirit. If there are any areas of bitterness in my heart, I ask You to reveal them to me so that I can release them to You, and You can transform my mind. I realize now that I have held onto unmet expectations. Help me to release them to You and trust that You will work all things for good. I ask these things in the precious name of Jesus. Amen.

CHAPTER 8

Benefits of Forgiveness

There is strong biblical support for the necessity of forgiveness. Matthew 6:14–15 says, "For if you forgive others their trespasses, your heavenly Father will also forgive you, but if you do not forgive others their trespasses, neither will your Father forgive your trespasses."

When we refuse to forgive others, we cut ourselves off from personal forgiveness from the Lord. We may be able to live without the forgiveness of others, but we cannot live without the forgiveness of God. After God forgives us for our sins, and then we refuse to forgive others, we walk away from the Lord's protection. Out of the Lord's shelter is a dangerous place to be.

In the Parable of the Unforgiving Servant, recorded in Matthew 18:23–35, Jesus gave a poignant example of a servant who owed an enormous debt to his master that he could not pay. He begged the master not to sell him and his family. The master generously released him from the large debt. Then that same person found one of his servants who owed him a small debt. He refused to release his servant of the minor debt and instead sent him to prison. When the master heard what had happened, he summoned the man he released from the debt, calling him wicked because he did not have mercy on his fellow servant. The master sent his servant to jail until he could pay the enormous debt because of his unforgiveness. Through this parable, Jesus warns us that we will suffer terrible consequences if we do not forgive others from our hearts.

Forgiveness is vital to the Lord. God sent His only Son to pay the price for our sins, so there would be no barrier of sin between God and us. We have done nothing to deserve this. The Lord's sacrifice was not based on our merit but instead on God's mercy, love, grace, and compassion for us. Jesus looked down at the men who were crucifying Him, and He said, "Father, forgive them, for they know not what they do." (See Luke 23:34.) Jesus expressed the compassion He wants us to have when we forgive others.

We are called to show grace to others by forgiving them when they do not deserve it, just as the Lord forgives us when we do not merit it. In all my years in church, I heard that God's grace was getting what we do not deserve, and His mercy is not getting what we do deserve.

There are consequences when we choose to allow an unforgiving spirit to reign in us. Unforgiveness prevents God's blessing in our lives. Kendall suggests that when we refuse to forgive, God stands back and lets us cope with our own problems. We are essentially asking God to step aside because we want to be the judge and jury. He can then treat us as an enemy. Unforgiveness can grieve the Holy Spirit.[6] We need the Holy Spirit in our lives to convict us of God's truth and comfort us. We do not want to alienate ourselves from the Lord.

Most people do not realize that forgiveness brings God's blessings and freedom. The greatest gift we receive when we commit our life to Jesus is our guaranteed inheritance with Him, God, and the Holy Spirit in eternity. We do not need to wait until eternity to enjoy all the blessings God has for us now as His chosen and adopted children.

God's blessings are available now. Through daily conversations, prayer, and journaling, we can enjoy intimacy with the Lord as our closest friend and confidant. We no longer need to navigate life on our own because the Lord walks with us. He carries us through the tough times and gives us strength. In our intimate relationship with the Lord, we gain an understanding of God's purpose in our lives, and we become more like Jesus. We recognize we are rich because we have received Christ's righteousness, power, and authority. This richness is not the same wealth the world embraces as money or promotion. That wealth will fade away and be left behind when we leave our earthly homes.

Press and I saw the positive results of forgiveness in the lives of the people we met in prayer. I taught graduate education courses in the Caribbean on three separate occasions to students completing a Master's degree in special education. Press came with me each time. He worked online at our motel teaching business courses for Liberty University while I taught on the Caribbean college campus. During our last visit to the island, he spoke with a staff person at the motel and felt led to ask her if she would like to receive prayer. She promised to think about this request and get back to him. She returned the next day to say that she would like us to pray with her the following day at the end of her shift.

She arrived at our room around 4:30 p.m. We listened to her concerns and asked her what she would like the Lord to heal. She said she had lived with a man for nine years who physically abused her, but she broke off that relationship two years earlier. Her eyes filled with tears while we led her through a prayer to forgive him for the abuse and ask the Lord for forgiveness for her part in the relationship. She also said a relative physically abused her when she was much younger.

After listening to several other painful stories for an hour, we prayed for the Lord to heal her broken heart and bring Godly people into her life. She appeared joyful, and her countenance reflected a sense of peace at the end of the prayer session. She told us that after she forgave her abusers, she felt inner turmoil and agitation melt away. We assured her that we would continue to pray for her when we returned home since we were leaving the following day.

As we put our suitcases at the motel entrance to prepare to ride to the airport in the morning, someone yelled my name and exclaimed that she had to talk with me—the woman we prayed with the evening before. She excitedly told us how good God had been to her. She said she walked to the bus stop right after the prayer session. The relative who had physically abused her years earlier was driving past and offered to drive her home. She had not seen him in years, and he did not live in the bus stop area, so she was puzzled why he was in that area of the island. They were able to reconcile their relationship on the drive to her house.

She believed God intervened and arranged the meeting with her relative. More divine appointments awaited her when she arrived home that evening. Her twenty-year-old grandson sat in her living room and jumped up to greet her with a kiss when she entered the room. He had been living with her previously but moved out several months earlier. She worried about him and had been concerned about his welfare. Now she felt relieved to see him in person and hear that he wanted to live with her again. An hour later, her daughter contacted her to reconcile their relationship.

We embraced each other with tears in our eyes and marveled at the goodness of God. When we prayed with her, I truly believed God would heal her, but I had not imagined He would do it immediately and heal multiple broken relationships. His plan was bigger and better than what I imagined might happen.

Then she said she thought God purposely sent us to the Caribbean to be part of her healing. At that moment, I believed our prayer time was a divine appointment orchestrated by God to bless not only her, but also me and Press. We were excited to see how God would use us next.

Pray this prayer aloud:

> Lord, I ask You to help me to see others the way that You see them. Help me to extend grace as You have shown us in the Bible so that I can forgive them. I ask for divine appointments to engage with others to extend compassion and kindness as You did. I want to be Jesus with skin on to a hurting world. Thank you for forgiving me for not pardoning those I needed to forgive in the past. I want the Holy Spirit in my life and the blessings that forgiveness brings. Thank you, Lord, for forgiving me and removing my sins as far as the east is from the west. Amen.

CHAPTER 9

Releasing Ourselves and God

Many people find it more difficult to forgive themselves than to forgive others. We must understand the importance of forgiving ourselves and not feel guilty about doing so.

Press and I have prayed with people who said they could not forgive themselves because they believed they deserved punishment. This refusal could be considered a form of self-hatred and may be rooted in pride. It also means they assumed the role of judge, which only belongs to God.

These prayer recipients may have deserved punishment. But the Bible assures us sin confessed to God is completely forgiven. We are not supposed to look back with regret at our mistakes after we confess them and ask for forgiveness. Feeling guilt over wrongdoings confessed to the Lord is false guilt and is not from God. In Joel 2:25, God promises to take the wasted years stolen from us and restore them. God does not change, and He keeps His promises. He will do the same for us today.

Press and I have heard others say forgiving yourself is selfish. Kendall asserts that not forgiving yourself is a selfish act because then we do not love ourselves the way God intended.[7]

When I gave presentations explaining inner healing at the prison facility, I told the men once they sincerely ask the Lord for forgiveness for their misdeeds, He will absolve them. Jesus promises us in 1 John 1:9 that "he is faithful and just to forgive us our sins and to cleanse us from all unrighteousness." They are new creations and washed clean after confession. Based on 1 John 1:9, Jesus is not keeping a rap sheet on them when they acknowledge their transgressions and repent. I often shared this scripture with the men in the prison.

I became aware I could not wholly apply this promise to myself. I still experienced periodic false guilt, shame, and condemnation for past mistakes. These feelings were not from the Lord. The Holy Spirit does convict us of God's truth, but He does not shame us. Shame and condemnation are ploys of the enemy when we believe his lies about ourselves.

As I continued to preach at the prison, the Holy Spirit showed me I needed to take hold of 1 John 1:9 for myself. In addition, 2 Corinthians 5:17 says, "Therefore, if anyone is in Christ, he is a new creation. The old has passed away; behold, the new has come." I am a new creation, and I needed to start living my life in this reality. I knew I had not done anything so hideous to be deemed unforgivable. My heart needed to embrace this fully. If the Lord forgave me for my transgressions, and I knew He did once I confessed them, then what right did I have continuing to hold on to them? I needed to let go of my pride.

I was horrified when I recognized my reluctance to forgive myself could be related to pride. I did not view myself as a prideful person and found this possibility very distressing. The thought I inadvertently could be telling the Lord to step out of the way because I could handle this myself was absurd.

I also heard others say this refusal to release ourselves suggests we believe Jesus's dying on the cross for our sins was not enough. I knew I needed to repent for holding on to what God had already absolved. It was inconceivable and appalling to think Jesus's ultimate sacrifice on the cross was not sufficient. When we refuse to let go of what the Lord already forgave, isn't this the implication? In essence, when we continue to hang on to the guilt and condemnation God already cleansed, we refuse to enjoy what He freely gave us. This refusal is dishonoring to God.

Anger Toward God

We sometimes struggle with our feelings toward God when bad things happen to us. We may believe He should have prevented these circumstances. I often have heard people say, "If He is truly a loving God, He would not have allowed this to happen to me." Others have gone as far as to say then they could not believe in a God who allowed terrible things to happen to them.

In reality, God does not need forgiveness because He is holy, and He does not sin. This does not negate the fact that the anger, disappointment, or resentment we feel toward Him when we are hurt rob us of a peaceful, loving relationship with Father God. These reactions may indicate that we have a distorted image of God. We must realize God loves us, regardless of how we feel about Him. The New Testament and the Old Testament contain numerous passages with His promise never to leave or forsake us. I met many people who were either unaware of these promises or had forgotten them when pain and disappointment filled their daily lives.

In my role as a school psychologist, I worked with parents who described feeling isolated and abandoned while struggling to meet their child's special needs. Their need for assistance and encouragement led Press and I to start a support group for parents of children with autism spectrum disorders in 2000. We wanted to share what we had learned to help parents and family members access resources and find support on this journey filled with many potholes. We did not want them to experience the loneliness and isolation we had endured when we navigated the medical and educational systems several years earlier.

We had the privilege of meeting many dedicated parents who were their children's best advocates. We also heard many heart-wrenching stories. Mothers told us they lost friends, relatives, and spouses because of their child's disability. Many of their children could not speak, and the mothers grieved because they would never hear their children say, "I love you." Parents were exhausted from the never-ending battles with their school districts to access the services their children needed, but the school districts refused to provide.

65

We heard parents say they needed to become hardened to prepare for each day's battles and the inevitable phone call from the school saying their child's behavior was again out of control.

The dark circles under their eyes and the lines on their faces bore evidence of many sleepless nights. Fear etched in their voices when they expressed concern over the well-being of their other children. The intense needs of their child on the autism spectrum and the demand for their mother's time frequently meant siblings had to take care of themselves. Medical bills and daily living expenses strained the family's already tight budgets. Often, if there were two parents at home, one of the parent's jobs was in jeopardy over missed time at work to take care of their child with autism.

The difficulties suffered left several parents questioning why God would allow this to happen to them. They wondered why He was punishing them. Some parents said their church would not allow their children to participate in services because of their unpredictable behavior. Feeling alone and abandoned, they lashed out at God.

Press and I listened to their concerns and assured them that God had big shoulders and could handle anything they wanted to hurl at Him. We explained that we do not always know why challenging situations happen on this side of Heaven.

Many parents received comfort hearing the stories of other families in similar situations. They no longer felt isolated. They found others to talk with who understood their grief. Often, parents shared practical solutions to problems they faced. Parents encouraged each other and checked on each other in between support group meetings. Over several months, their anger dissipated, and many of the parents talked about the unexpected positives they experienced because of having a child with a disability. They would never have met some of the people they now enjoyed socializing with in the support group. Others said they learned what was important in life, and their values changed. Others thanked God for the opportunity to draw closer to Him when they were at the end of their rope. Several held onto the Lord's promise to turn all things to good.

Consider asking God in prayer if you are holding any anger, resentment, bitterness, or disappointment with Him for something in your past. If the

Lord reveals a memory or a hurt you are carrying, ask Him if there is something you need to surrender to Him. Tell Him how you feel. Those feelings need to be brought to the light for the Lord to heal. Remember, He always loves you. Give Him all your negative feelings. Jesus already paid for all your pain at the cross 2,000 years ago, so give it all back to Him. It is His, and He does not want you to carry it any longer.

Now What?

As Christians, we need to realize forgiveness is not an option for us—it is a command. Jesus said in John 20:23, "If you forgive the sins of any, they are forgiven them; if you withhold forgiveness from any, it is withheld." Ask the Lord for His grace to help forgive yourself and your offenders. We need to deal with offenses immediately, so we do not give the enemy a foothold. The first step is recognizing when we feel wronged. Then, we need to quickly take that offense to Jesus to ask Him to help us.

The following suggestions can guide you in forgiveness:

- First, recognize that you feel offended.

- If bitterness has set in, remove its legal right to remain by quickly confessing this to Jesus. You do not want to give the enemy a reason to stay. Shut that door.

- Quickly choose to forgive the offender. The offender could be yourself. Remember, forgiveness is not a feeling. It is a choice. If you struggle to forgive, ask the Lord for His help.

- Declare that you release the wrongdoer from any debt you believe they owe you.

- Repent for judging the person(s) who wounded you and release all judgments you made against them.

- Visualize taking the offender off your hook and placing them on Jesus's hook. You want to turn the person and the situation completely over to Jesus to deal with as He will.

- Ask the Lord to renew your mind, especially if you allowed bitterness to take root. He can help you dismantle old thoughts and replace them with new ones. He can restore what you lost after surrendering your right to hang on to unforgiveness.

- Ask the Lord for His truth and compassion in this situation. Ask Him to show you how He sees the offender and for His help to bless that person.

Given the understanding that forgiveness is a lifestyle practiced daily, we need to recognize God forgives us of our sins when we forgive others who wound us. We should adopt this into our daily prayer life. Jesus says in Mark 11:25, "And whenever you stand praying, forgive, if you have anything against anyone, so that your Father also who is in heaven may forgive you your trespasses." Peter asked Jesus if he needed to forgive someone who sinned against him as many as seven times. Jesus replied in Matthew 18:22, "I do not say to you seven times, but seventy-seven times." The implication here is this refers to limitless forgiveness rather than a legalistic formula.

Pray this prayer aloud:

> Lord, I recognize there were times when I held onto self-condemnation even after I knew You forgave me for my mistakes. I had no right to hold on to what You already absolved. I repent for believing the lies of the enemy that kept me from walking in Your freedom. Thank you for sending Jesus to be the ultimate sacrifice for my sins. Forgive me for when I vented my anger on You. Thank you for Your promise in Psalm 103 to remove my sins "as far as the east is from the west." Please bring to my mind any others I am holding unforgiveness toward so I can release them and receive Your forgiveness and peace. Amen.

SECTION 4

Lies

Many people are unaware that to some extent they live out of incorrect beliefs. These lies about ourselves, others, and God affect our perceptions and behaviors. We can ask the Lord to reveal any lies we have believed. This appeal could be as simple as asking Jesus, "What lies(s) have I believed?" or "Which lie do you want to talk with me about now?" You can do this through prayer, conversations with the Lord, or journaling. Invite Him to show you His truth.

CHAPTER 10

Not Good Enough

Believing you are not good enough is the enemy's lie to hold you back from God's plans for your life. We all have a destiny and a God-given purpose.

Psalm 139:16 tells us God planned us, and He saw us before we were born. He recorded our days in His book, with every moment laid out before a single day had passed. Ephesians 1:11–12 tells us because we are united with Christ, "In him we have obtained an inheritance." He chose us in advance, and He makes everything work out according to His plan. When we understand and embrace our spiritual power and authority in Christ, we live in freedom and joy. The enemy wants us to remain unaware of this power and authority. He is afraid we would walk into our God-given calling if we realize our strength in Christ.

In my early twenties, self-condemnation, fear, and anxiety resurfaced. Over ten years earlier, I had struggled for almost one year with the fear of dying. I used to pray the following childhood prayer fervently each evening: "Now I lay me down to sleep, I pray the Lord my soul to keep; If I should die before I wake, I pray the Lord my soul to take." Then a little over a decade later, I was afraid of where I would be going after I died. I compared myself to others, and I always seemed to come up short in my eyes. I had high and unrealistic expectations and judged myself harshly.

I believed the enemy's lie that I was not good enough to go to Heaven. I had not shared this concern with anyone, not even my husband of three years. Despite attending church my whole life, I did not understand it was not my works and good deeds that would get me to Heaven. I didn't understand that we can never be sufficient or measure up on our own. What matters is our faith in Christ, who already paid the price for our sins.

I desperately wanted to please God, so I continued volunteering my time to help others, thinking this pleased Him. It did not occur to me then to ask God if these activities were what He wanted me to do. I was so focused on trying to be good enough that I nearly wore myself out.

Despite all my efforts, I never felt convinced that I measured up. I did not realize I probably served the Lord from the wrong heart motives. Although assisting others gave me a sense of worth, fear and guilt were the driving forces instead of joy and thankfulness for all the Lord had done for me. I would soon find out more about God's love for me during the summer of 1976.

My brother, Kerry, invited us to attend his wedding in August 1976. I flew to Florida with my infant son for the occasion. Press needed to remain in Dayton, Ohio, to complete his duties before his upcoming separation from the Air Force. I stayed at my parents' home, which was in the same town as the wedding, hoping to have an opportunity to talk with Kerry privately about my current anxiety before his big day.

Several days before my arrival, I discovered a small lump in the axilla area under my arm, which left me nervous. My overriding fear was this could be cancer, and I might miss spending eternity in Heaven because I was not acceptable.

Kerry and I grew up together until I left home in 1970 to go to college. The following year Kerry joined the Navy. He was overseas and unable to come home in 1973 for my wedding. Just fifteen months younger, Kerry was more of a risk-taker and somewhat more rebellious than I ever was.

After Kerry came back to the United States on leave from the Navy, he seemed different. He was not like the brother I knew growing up. Kerry certainly was no longer rebellious, and he appeared more self-confident and unrestrained. He looked relaxed, and he did not seem preoccupied with being good enough.

I wanted the peace he seemed to carry. I wanted to be free of worry, fear, and anxiety. I thought about some of the less than virtuous choices he had made earlier while I continued to try my hardest to please God and others. And yet, he found a sense of peace I was unable to attain. That certainly did not seem fair.

Kerry explained to me one night that he had changed because he decided to surrender his life to Jesus. At that time, I did not understand what it meant to have a personal relationship with Jesus. After all, I was too busy trying to gain validation and please God. I did not realize God already loved me, and I did not need to earn His love. All I needed to do was turn my life over to Him completely. My efforts to measure up to some standard were not the basis of His love for me. It would still be a while before I ultimately realized striving for approval needed to stop.

My First Awareness of the Holy Spirit

Kerry was busy getting ready for his wedding in Florida that August, so he did not have time to speak with me privately as I hoped he would. I decided to go to Kerry's Assembly of God church with my younger brother the evening before the wedding. The service was much different from the services I was familiar with growing up in Presbyterian churches. That evening Kerry's friend, Bill, spoke to me at the end of the service. I had not met Bill before that night.

Bill said the Holy Spirit told him I was concerned about going to Heaven. I leaned back in my pew, biting my lip. How could he know that? I had not disclosed this overwhelming fear to anyone. I was aware that the Holy Spirit is part of the Trinity, but I had not given much thought to Him being active in our lives.

The Holy Spirit undoubtedly pursued me. When I gained my composure, Bill offered to pray with me at my parents' home and explain salvation in Jesus that evening.

Bill prayed at the kitchen table with my mother and me while my father quietly sat observing. Bill explained that we all sin and fall short of the glory of God. God provided redemption for us through Jesus Christ because He loves us so much and does not want anyone to perish. Bill said that the moment we give our hearts to Jesus and put our complete trust in Him, God promises to forgive our sins and grant us eternal life. We simply need to confess our sins, repent, and invite Jesus into our hearts.

My father's glasses rested toward the bottom of his nose, leaving his eyes gazing out above the top rim of his glasses. He maintained this contemplative pose while my mother and I listened to Bill's explanation of the plan of salvation supported by Scripture. Then we eagerly, with tears in our eyes, asked Jesus to be the Lord of our lives.

We noticed what appeared to be hints of skepticism in my father's facial expressions. He struggled with the salvation plan because it seemed so simple and too good to be true. Nothing came easy in my father's life, and he always worked hard. He accepted the belief you need to pull yourself up by your bootstraps, and he taught this to his children. I understood much later this came from embracing what is known as an orphan lifestyle.

My father lived with several aunts and uncles after his mother died when he was ten years old. He wore out his welcome by frequently misbehaving, which resulted in several different placements among family members. He described this as being bounced out of one home and into another. My dad was raised in the Catholic faith and educated in Catholic schools. Although he understood God sent Jesus to die for our sins, he believed in the importance of our works and good deeds to earn salvation.

Toward the end of our evening with Bill, my father asked if he could pose a hypothetical question. He wanted to know if someone spent their entire life drinking, carousing with women, and cheating others, and then accepted Jesus on their deathbed, would they still go to Heaven to spend eternity with the Lord. Bill emphatically said, "Yes." Horrified, my father slammed his fist on the table, loudly saying, "That is not fair!"

Looking back on this memory, I realize, of course, it seems unreasonable. But conversely, is it fair that Jesus suffered a terrible crucifixion for us? No, it is not. But it demonstrates the great lengths God will go to make sure His children will be with Him for eternity. In 2 Peter 3:9, we read that God is not willing that any should perish but rather that all would come to repentance. Jesus said after He left, He would send the Holy Spirit to be with us, comfort, encourage, and guide us. (See John 15 and 16.)

When I returned home to Ohio after Kerry's wedding, Press immediately noticed a change in my countenance. He asked me for the details regarding what happened in Florida because I looked much calmer and more at peace than when I left home. I explained what happened and how my mother and I accepted Jesus as our Lord and Savior. More rejoicing came later that week when the doctor said the small lump under my arm was nothing to be concerned about—only a swollen sweat gland.

I could not wait to tell our church friends about my experience in Florida. The hymns I previously sang for years now looked different when I participated in Sunday worship services. It seemed as though the Lord gave me fresh eyes to see meanings and glimpses of eternal life in the hymns that I had not noticed earlier. I shared my exhilaration over being saved with our pastor. He told me our denomination did not believe in being saved because we are always in the process of working out our salvation. This response did not deter my enthusiasm over my newfound relationship with the Lord. Although years later, I would find myself again believing the lie that I did not qualify for Heaven.

For the next fifteen years, I actively served in church teaching children and volunteering for fund-raising activities, while also attending Bible study classes for my personal growth. Church sermons focused on God's love for us, but there was no mention of how the Holy Spirit speaks to us. I put the Holy Spirit on a shelf while I took charge of my life and worked tirelessly to gain God's approval again. I had forgotten that I did not need to earn the Lord's approval. He already loved me and had pursued me. He sent Bill to speak with me about the Holy Spirit and God's love for me over a decade earlier.

When we moved to Kansas City in 1990, I met women at church who introduced me to Stonecroft Ministries, a Christian organization that equips and encourages women to share the gospel of Jesus with their communities.

This encounter opened my eyes to what it meant to have a personal relationship with the Lord. My new friend told me that she had an experience similar to mine when she first encountered the Holy Spirit. Her previous church did not talk much about the Holy Spirit or the importance of walking with Him daily. She had no one with whom she could share her new relationship with the Lord at that time. She again used the words "personal relationship" with the Lord when she spoke about Jesus. I desperately wanted to know the Lord more deeply and understand what this personal connection looked like.

I joined a Stonecroft Ministries Bible study and also attended the Experiencing God Bible study written by pastor and author Henry Blackaby. I learned that the Holy Spirit relentlessly pursues us but does not force Himself on anyone. We all have free will, and we decide if we will receive the Lord's blessings in our lives. I did not need to work tirelessly to try and figure out what volunteer activities the Lord wanted me to do. Blackaby teaches that God is at work all around us and invites us to join Him. I just needed to ask Him where He wanted me to serve, and I would come to know and experience the Lord when I obeyed. I sensed a reawakening of the Holy Spirit in me that had remained dormant.

My relationship with the Lord was ignited further when I became involved in inner healing prayer in 2011. I experienced a deeper awareness of the Holy Spirit that resides in me and partners with me. Finally, I understood that the Lord is speaking to us all the time. I just needed to tune in and listen. He speaks to us through the Bible, others, and the church. He speaks to us personally through thoughts, pictures, visions, dreams, and circumstances.

Pray this prayer aloud:

> God, thank you that I do not need to strive to be good enough or measure up to someone else's standard. Forgive me for believing the enemy's lies that I am not good enough. I only need to focus on what You think of me. You adopted me into Your family when I accepted Jesus as my Lord and Savior. I am good enough because Jesus resides in me. Your Word tells me I have been equipped and empowered to do all You have called me to do. Help me each day to trust in Your promises. Amen.

CHAPTER II

Generational Patterns and Shame

Although the Holy Spirit powerfully met me in 1976 and then again fifteen years later, I became distracted at times and did not fully embrace all the Lord had given me. Inner healing prayer taught me that I had believed lies about myself and the Lord that sidetracked me.

The Lord is gracious, and He placed people in my life to walk alongside me and help nurture our relationship, which evolved over forty years. I learned most of my beliefs about justice in my parents' home. They learned how to judge fairness from their upbringing. We were unaware of the generational pattern of withholding forgiveness until justice prevailed. What I accepted as fact was not accurate.

I erroneously assumed life was supposed to be fair. We are not guaranteed a problem-free life as I once believed. Living as a self-reliant person trying to measure up to some self-imposed standard is not God's plan. We need to rely on God for everything. We are good enough because Christ dwells in us when we make Him the Lord of our lives. No amount of righteous works will ensure a fair life on earth. Neither will outstanding deeds earn us a place in Heaven if we do not believe in Jesus.

I am not blaming my parents or others who influenced me in my growing-up years. I forgave my parents many years ago for the misunderstandings, and I also asked their forgiveness for the ways I treated them poorly and dishonored them. The point here is we all have generational patterns and false beliefs in our family lines that may not correctly align with God's reality. When we become aware of them, we can repent for our part in agreeing with any associated lies, ask for forgiveness, and invite the Lord to share His truth. He will tell us if we ask and listen to His answer. His reply may come in the form of thoughts, a vision, a dream, or words from another person.

Another lie I believed was that if people truly knew me, they would reject me. My parents frequently told me they did not understand me in my teen years. They said that if others got to know me, they would not want me. They jokingly said they did not know where I came from because I was so unlike them. I loved academics and excelled in school, and they told me schoolwork did not come easy for them. They could not relate to my excitement for academic study. I received a lot of praise from my teachers and friends at school, so I continued to work hard at excelling scholastically. I did not sense this positive reinforcement for my efforts at home.

I tried hard to figure out what I could do to make family life more harmonious because I was aware of an underlying tension at home. Being good and doing well in school were not working to bring harmony. Rebelling, as my brothers did, seemed to garner attention, but I chose not to rebel. I did not realize there were negative generational patterns at work that needed breaking.

Later in life, I learned these influences included abandonment, addiction, shame, fear, control, and an orphan lifestyle. Fortunately, I had encouraging relationships with my aunts and uncles, teachers, and several close friends during my childhood and teen years that provided some diversion from the stress at home.

During my teen years, I asked my parents questions concerning our purpose in life, searching for spiritual answers regarding the meaning of life and our God-given destiny. My parents thought my queries were odd, and they did not know how to respond. They told me they were just trying to get through each day. I later recognized they truly struggled to get through the challenges they faced each day and were not concerned with eternal matters.

My father battled with alcoholism, and my mother desperately tried to keep this family secret from getting out. My father did recover at the end of my sophomore year in college. I also accepted Press's wedding proposal that same summer. We married the following summer and relocated 700 miles away, where Press served in the Air Force. Several years later, my father became a sponsor to help others suffering from this addiction through Alcoholics Anonymous.

In my early adult years, my parents did ask for my forgiveness concerning the hurtful comments they spoke to me as a teenager. I did forgive them. They also shared some of the cruel statements their parents said to them that led to their frustration and distress. A generational pattern associated with emotional wounding existed. I was unaware of healing prayer and the power and authority I had to break those negative influences until later.

Sharing my feelings openly with my parents as an adult was beneficial and helped facilitate forgiveness and reconciliation. I did not realize I still believed the lie something was inherently wrong with me, and if others got to see the real me, they would reject me. Logically, this did not make sense. My friends got to know me well, and they accepted me. They were incredibly affirming. I appeared happy and successful to most others.

Reflecting on this time in my twenties and thirties, I think I stayed busy focusing on my marriage, raising my children, and my schoolwork and job, so these negative feelings and fears remained buried. They must have been buried alive because they resurfaced years later.

When I received healing prayer for myself in my later adult years, I remembered what my parents said decades earlier about people not wanting me once they knew me. I told the prayer minister I knew this was a lie. I thought this was dealt with when I forgave my parents decades earlier. At that moment, I realized that a part of me still believed I was fatally flawed and feared rejection if exposed. My head knowledge confirmed this was a lie, but my heart had not fully embraced this.

I told my prayer minister that my family members were experts at keeping secrets. My mother used to say her mom taught her "not to air her dirty laundry out for others to see," meaning do not share family secrets outside the home. My mother's sister, her only sibling, came to our house each weekday to talk and have tea with my mother during my growing-up years. Many years later, my aunt told me how she had no idea that my father struggled with alcoholism, despite being in our home each day. My mother never mentioned my father's drinking or why he needed to take sick days from work until she thought she had no other option.

I was away at college in the spring of 1971 when my mother needed someone to watch my younger brother when she accompanied my father to the hospital. My father had decided that he needed professional help to deal with his addiction and voluntarily signed himself into a hospital program. My mother had never hired a babysitter for her children, so she was in a quandary. She needed to make a quick decision while my father was motivated to seek help, so she called her sister. My mother could barely make eye contact with her sister because of her embarrassment in explaining the situation.

This request led to the unveiling of the family secret. Years later, my aunt told me that she feared my father had a heart attack or a severe illness when my mother approached her to care for my brother. Completely unaware of his addiction, my aunt expressed relief that it was only a hospitalization for rehabilitation and not a life-threatening condition.

I later realized keeping a lid on family secrets was an effort to cover the family's perceived shame. The shame resulted in fear over the possibility of exposure and embarrassment. This opened a door for the spirits of control and pride to operate. In this case, control involved managing people and situations to keep shame and secrets hidden. In my healing prayer session, the Lord showed me that I still believed I had a hidden, fatal flaw. I, nevertheless, did not know what the weakness was. I indeed feared it existed and might be connected to not being good enough. Was this another family secret hidden from me?

I believe the Lord purposely highlighted this situation that day because He wanted me to deal with this once and for all and experience His freedom. I asked for forgiveness for accepting the lie others would not want me if they knew me, and I asked Him to tell me what He wanted me to know.

The Lord said that I was His beloved daughter, and I was not fatally flawed. This divine revelation left me in awe. The Lord called me His treasured daughter—my real identity. Whatever imperfections I had imagined were irrelevant. As a result of my healing, I recognized that buried feelings do resurface and need to be brought into the Lord's light for Him to reveal His truth. Press and I observed that many people we prayed with also tried to bury their pain. This left them bound in chains until they received healing.

After Press and I prayed with several hundred people in individual healing prayer sessions, we also noticed repetitive patterns in the lies people believed. Although their life stories were different, they had similar false beliefs. Before I received healing prayer, I embraced many of the same lies we saw others struggle with. Not feeling good enough or acceptable to God was a common lie both men and women embraced.

Many of the men who requested prayer through the prison ministry believed this lie. They often expressed fear that God could never forgive them for what they did, and they could never measure up. They regretted their mistakes and thought they were unpardonable.

If these men experienced emotional wounds from their relationships with their earthly fathers, they frequently felt distant from Father God or fearful He would punish them. The majority of the men had fathers who deserted the family, and many had been abusive. This abandonment impacted their ability to trust and relate to Father God. They saw their fathers leave, reject, or abuse them or their mother and siblings. They felt God would do the same.

During our healing prayer sessions, the Holy Spirit showed them that they were beloved sons of the Lord. Their countenance and demeanor visibly changed once they offered their hurts to the Lord, and He mended their broken hearts. The men sensed Father God would never leave or abandon them. We often heard the men say they felt lighter and freer after the Lord met with them.

These prayer sessions brought Press and I much joy when we watched the Lord work in their lives. The Lord allowed us to participate in their transformation. We were not doing the healing, but we helped facilitate their restoration. We listened to the Holy Spirit for direction while we prayed for each man. The Holy Spirit frequently revealed something to share with the person. The Lord was doing the healing. Our friend, Dr. James Lee, describes this process by saying our Lord Jesus is the Great Physician, and we are just his nurses or assistants.

We observed that the people we prayed with believed lies about God and how He felt about them. They also believed lies about themselves, their relationships with others, and their future. We began to incorporate author Sharon Jaynes's four Rs in dealing with lies:

1. "Realize the enemy's true identity." Remember, John 10:10 tells us he has come to steal, kill, and destroy, but Jesus has come to give us a full life.

2. "Recognize the lies." John 8:32 says, "the truth will set you free." We need to become aware we have held onto mistaken beliefs and identify them.

3. "Reject the lies." 2 Corinthians 10:3–4 tells us the battles we fight are spiritual. We need to reject and renounce the lies we have acknowledged.

4. "Replace the lies with truth." Philippians 4:8 encourages us to meditate on what is true and honorable. We need to start seeing ourselves the way God sees us. Ask the Lord to show you His reality and how He sees you.[1]

Pray this prayer aloud:

> Lord, I ask You to reveal any open doors that have allowed the enemy access to plant lies that have caused shame and doubt. Thank you for Your promise to set the captives free. I forgive my ancestors for any lies they believed that gave the enemy a legal right in our family line. I am grateful that You are active in my life and want me to know Your truth. Amen.

CHAPTER 12

Lies about God and Ourselves

M any people told us they could never do enough to please God no matter how hard they tried. They assumed His love was either conditional based on their behavior or withheld. When they recognized their acceptance of a false image of God and asked for forgiveness for partnering with the lie that God wanted revenge, the Lord shared His truth with them. We asked them to find Bible verses that supported what the Lord showed them and mediate on them for homework.

For example, they told us the following:

- **Lie**: "I am not good enough to be loved by God."

- **God's Truth**: "I am good enough because Christ and the Holy Spirit dwell in me. John 1:12 tells me I am a child of God. 1 Corinthians 2:16 tells me I have the mind of Christ. Ephesians 1:3 tells me I have been blessed with every spiritual blessing."

Still, others believed God always judged them, and they were afraid to relax or else He would punish them. They did not know how to rest in the Lord.

- **Lie**: "God only loves me when I am busy doing good things."

- **God's Truth**: "I do not need to strive. I just need to lean into the Lord, and He will guide my path. The Lord says His yoke is light, and His burden is easy. I will find my rest in Him, according to Matthew 11:28–30. In Exodus 33:14, God promises to go with His people and to give them rest. He will do the same for me today."

Some people believed God loved others more than He loved them. They continually compared themselves to others and thought God had favorites.

- **Lie**: "God does not love me as much as He loves others."

- **God's Truth**: "I am a child of the Lord of the universe. Romans 8:39 says nothing can separate me from the love of God that is in Christ Jesus."

Others said they could not trust God because He let bad things happen to them, and He might do that again.

- **Lie**: "I cannot trust God who let bad things happen to my family and friends."

- **God's Truth**: "We live in a fallen world where people have free will and sometimes make bad choices that impact others. I do not need to fear because God promises all things to work together for good to those who love God, as stated in Romans 8:28. I can count on God's promises."

Via Zoom, we prayed with Melanie, who experienced several traumatic events in her life, including abuse. She felt remorseful over previous mistakes she made in response to the trauma endured, and she asked the Lord for forgiveness for these behaviors.

Although she believed the Lord forgave her, she recognized that she continued to feel distant from Father God. She tearfully told us she wanted a closer relationship with Him. Melanie thought her beliefs about God and her inability to trust Him might have stemmed from her unhealthy relationship with her stepfather. She forgave her stepfather when we prayed together.

During our prayer session, Melanie identified three lies she believed about God. She asked the Lord to shed His light on those beliefs and disclose His truth to her. Melanie shared the following ungodly beliefs and the truth she sensed from the Lord. She then found Bible verses to support God's truth and mediated on them until we met again.

- **Lie**: "Father God does not love me."

- **God's Truth**: "I am loved by the Lord. I am loveable. I am created in His image. He is love, and I am love. Colossians 3:12 tells me I am chosen by God, holy, and dearly loved."

- **Lie**: "I can't rest in the Lord. He'll treat me the way others treated me."

- **God's Truth:** "I have a rightful place on the Father's lap. 1 John 4:7–10 tells us God is love, and he sent His only Son into our world that we might live through Jesus."

- **Lie**: "God did not want to help me, and He did not care that they harmed me."

- **God's Truth:** "It was not okay with the Lord, and it grieved His Spirit. Isaiah 43:1 tells me God has redeemed me. Joel 2:25 declares God's promise to restore what the enemy has stolen. I can stand on that promise in my life. God restored Job after he experienced tremendous loss by giving him another ten children, increasing his wealth several-fold, and adding another 140 years to his life. He is restoring me."

Lies about Ourselves

One of the questions on our healing prayer interview form asks the prayer recipient if there were any past or present unkind words spoken to them or about them. When we met them for prayer, we explained that many people believe lies about themselves and their identity. They have held on to these viewpoints for a long time and assumed they were true. Several people shared destructive comments that focused on their physical attributes. Sometimes others told them negative things about themselves or their bodies. On other occasions, they spoke unkind words over themselves. We often heard people say the following:

"I am ugly" or "I will always be unattractive."

"I am fat. I will never be thin."

"I am dumb" or "I am stupid."

"I am doomed to have _(a specific disability)_ or _(illness)_. It is in my family genes."

During the prayer session, we asked the prayer recipient if they would be willing to ask the Lord for His truth regarding the belief that they shared with us. Almost every time they asked Jesus for His truth, they sensed His response either as a thought or a picture in their mind. Jesus showed them that they had believed a lie.

When they understood their belief was not accurate, they asked Jesus for His truth. Sometimes we suggested that they ask Jesus if He would convey how He sees them. The Lord shared His love for them and described how He viewed them each time they asked. Some people said they sensed the Lord thought they were beautiful. Others heard they were a precious jewel. Still, others heard God did not create junk, and they reflected His image. Others broke the lie illness was inevitable, and they received the Lord's gift of a healthy life.

Other falsehoods focused on personality attributes or their thoughts on their character. Sometimes the statements referred to self-worth. We heard comments such as:

"I am a loser" or "I am a failure."

"I always bring shame and disappointment."

"Something is wrong with me."

"I will never change."

"I'll never be happy" or "I don't deserve to be happy."

"I'll never get ahead."

"I am just average or uninteresting."

"I am worthless."

"I'll never be successful."

"My value is in what I do."

"I have to be strong."

"I have wasted a lot of time and energy and some of the best years of my life."

"I will always be _____" (often words in the blank were "fearful," "anxious," "insecure," or "powerless").

Each time, the Lord gave them a thought, word, or picture uniquely meaningful to them, and they perceived His love and His truth. Sometimes, He brought a Bible verse to mind that showed He valued them because they are His child. Even if their parents told them they were an accident, the Lord said they are not a mistake in His eyes. He knew them before their conception. Often, the Lord gave Press and I a word to speak to the person. I sensed the word "troubadour" when we prayed with a man in the prison. I was not sure how that word was relevant. When I told him, he excitedly exclaimed that he loved to sing. He now wanted to worship the Lord with song. We had no idea he enjoyed singing and worshipping until I shared that word with him.

On another occasion, we prayed for a young woman who experienced several failed relationships. I sensed the Lord wanted me to tell her she was "not trash." I did not say this at first because I thought it was a harsh comment. While we continued to pray with her, I sensed I was supposed to share this with her, even though I was uncomfortable. Internally I tried to negotiate with the Lord about this. I thought, Lord, you have to be kidding! You want me to tell her that? That is not uplifting. I thought we were supposed to encourage people.

As soon as I was obedient to what I believed the Lord wanted me to voice, she broke down in tears and said those were the exact words spoken to her that caused so much pain in her last relationship. When she released the pain held deep inside her heart, the Lord gave her peace and restored her.

Other lies focused on how the person related to others. We've heard:

"Everyone I love leaves me. I will never love anyone."

"I have to guard and hide my emotions and feelings."

"I have to protect my heart from others so that I do not get hurt again."

"No one understands me."

"I was meant to be alone."

"I'll never marry."

"I will never be a good spouse."

"I do not belong. I will always be left out."

"The best way to avoid rejection and hurt is to isolate myself."

In these situations, the Lord showed the person the truth through a picture they saw in their mind's eye or words that popped into their mind. They then understood how He was always with them, and He would never leave or abandon them. He healed their wounded hearts. We heard several people say, "It is difficult to describe how I know I heard from the Lord. I just know that I know the Lord loves me."

Still, other lies focused on the person's beliefs about their future and feelings of hopelessness. We've heard:

"I will never have money. I will always have financial problems."

"I will always have to work this hard."

"I can never get ahead."

"I do not deserve _____" (often words in the blank were "a good life," "happiness," or "God's love").

"My life is hopeless."

"I will never do anything right."

"I am a victim of circumstances."

"The Lord cannot use me because there is something not valuable about me."

"I can't forgive myself."

The Lord revealed the truth in a way the person would understand. Some people told us they sensed a warmth in their body and felt a peace that had not been there before we prayed. Others saw a memory in their mind where Jesus had provided for them. They were not lacking, nor did the Lord see them as victims. Several people were astonished by positive words that came into their minds.

I could relate to those who experienced difficulty forgiving themselves because I had struggled with this. Sometimes, this lie's root is pride that needs to be exposed, repented, and renounced. When people recognized that believing they could not forgive themselves was essentially saying Jesus's dying on the cross was not enough, they could reject this lie, request forgiveness, and ask the Holy Spirit to fill them with His blessings.

Do any of the lies shared by others sound familiar? Have you embraced some of these statements? If you are holding on to falsehoods, consider repeating this prayer from our manual, *Simple Effective Prayer: A Model for Inner Healing*, as a guide to dismantling false beliefs.

After you identify the lie, pray aloud the bolded words.

1. **I confess my sin of believing the lie that _____, and I forgive each of the following people for influencing me to form this false belief** (*Under the guidance of the Holy Spirit, name the people aloud*). **I choose to forgive _____, _____, _____, _____.**

2. **Lord, I ask You to forgive me for accepting this false belief and living my life based on it. I receive Your forgiveness, and I choose to forgive myself for believing this lie.**

3. **I renounce and break agreement with this false belief and any associated darkness.**

    Pause here and ask the Holy Spirit for the truth that replaces the false belief. You may ask the Lord aloud, **"What do You want me to believe about this situation or myself?"** *Use the information gained here to complete step 4.*

4. **I choose to accept, believe, and receive Your truth Lord, which is _____.**

We found it helpful to have the person breaking the lie take time afterward to find a Bible passage that shares the message the Lord revealed. We encouraged them to meditate daily on the verse for several weeks.

SECTION 5

Emotional Wounds

God uniquely and wonderfully created each person in His image with emotions and feelings. Sometimes, these emotions get distorted by the enemy, others, and our own thoughts, and our hearts become wounded. We have prayed with hundreds of people in our community and in the prison and found many dealt with similar emotional wounds. Although their life stories were different, they commonly expressed feelings of guilt, fear, anxiety, shame, anger, unworthiness, self-condemnation, rejection, and depression. Painful and distressing emotions, such as guilt and fear, may indicate areas in your life that need the Lord's touch. Do not bury them, but rather bring them into the light for the Lord to heal. He will heal your deepest wounds when you release them to Him. Ask Him to guard your heart.

CHAPTER 13

Your Feelings Aren't Right or Wrong

When I was in my early thirties, a colleague said to me, "Our feelings are not right or wrong. They simply are just our feelings." I realized I mistakenly judged some of my feelings and emotions as good and others as bad in contemplating this statement. This self-judgment led to extensive, relatively unsuccessful efforts to hide them.

The terms *emotions* and *feelings* are often used interchangeably. Some scientists and researchers view emotions as instinctual and occurring on the subconscious or unconscious level, whereas "feelings are the conscious experience of emotional reactions."[1] Feelings can be considered the labels we consciously place on the emotions we experience.

Feelings and Emotions Serve a Purpose

For most of my life, I did not grasp the idea that emotions are God-given and serve a purpose. Emotions help us understand ourselves and others. They can motivate us to set goals and act on those objectives if we recognize and acknowledge them instead of ignoring or burying them. For example, experiencing anxiety before final exams may spur us to study. Awareness of how we feel in different situations will lead us to participate in activities we enjoy and avoid activities that do not bring pleasure.

The Bible states God created us in His image. Wouldn't our emotions then be reflective of our Lord's? Why then would we try to negate or hide them? The Bible includes numerous passages referring to God's emotions.

1 Kings 3:10 refers to God being pleased.

Genesis 6:6 mentions God felt regret.

I Kings 11:9 indicates God was angry.

Similarly, we know Jesus experienced a range of emotions while on earth.

John 11:5 tells us Jesus loved Martha, her sister, and Lazarus.

Luke 10:21 says Jesus rejoiced in the Holy Spirit.

Luke 7:9 states He marveled at the centurion's faith.

Mark 1:41 says Jesus was moved with pity when cleansing the leper.

Jesus also felt distressing emotions.

Mark 3:5 states Jesus was angry and grieved at those watching to see if He would heal on the Sabbath.

Luke 22:44 describes the great agony Jesus endured at the Mount of Olives before His betrayal and arrest. His sweat became like large drops of blood falling to the ground.

Not everyone acknowledges emotions as God-given or beneficial. After praying with others, I observed that many people also tried to hide or negate their feelings due to shame and fear of criticism from others. Some people judged them as either right or wrong, or as good or bad, as I mistakenly did.

Often the beliefs we form regarding our emotions shape how we view the world. If accused of overreacting or reacting inappropriately in a situation, we may erroneously believe our emotions and feelings are harmful and cannot be trusted. Worse yet, we may accept the lie that we are inherently flawed. In actuality, our behavior or reaction to the emotion or feeling may be the issue.

I mistakenly thought I needed to judge my feelings until a younger college told me otherwise. We were brainstorming ways to diffuse emotionally charged situations at a summer church camp I directed. I knew how we acted in response to our feelings was important, but I had not fully realized the feelings themselves were not fundamentally right or wrong. There are acceptable ways to express uncomfortable feelings. We taught the counselors how to take responsibility for their feelings and communicate them without sarcasm or ridicule, so the person receiving their message still felt valued and respected. Teaching them how to do this reminded me to view my feelings and emotions as a signal to think about before reacting. Sometimes these feelings pointed to areas in my life in need of healing.

Looking back on my formative years, I realized my family members often did not take responsibility for their feelings and instead judged and blamed each other. Perhaps if we had correctly identified our emotions, we could have expressed them appropriately instead of hiding or negating them or using them to justify an inappropriate response.

I also interpreted my family's comments and reactions to mean certain emotions were wrong and should not be displayed—especially anger, sadness, and depression. I erroneously believed I should not have these emotions and tried hard to conceal them.

The irony was I often could not hide my moods. My facial expressions seemed to give away my feelings, and I thought my parents read me like "an open book." My parents continuously teased me for my numerous faces. Also, there were occasions when I was unaware that I was revealing a particular emotion or feeling.

A typical scenario at the dinner table began with my father pointing his finger at my face and saying something like, "There she goes with face number twenty-five." When I looked confused because I was not aware of my expression, he said something like, "Oh no! Now it is changing to number fifty-seven. Oh wait, here comes number forty-nine. Oh no, now that is followed by number twenty-seven." He said this while continuing to study my face and point at me. I became frustrated with this hurtful teasing, particularly when I did not realize I showed any feeling or emotion.

My father made up numbers to assign to my appearances each time he did this. He did not give one particular number to a specific facial expression.

The message I received was I had numerous faces, and this was not normal. I began to believe the lie something must inherently be wrong with me. Interestingly, my friends never teased me about this. They found it endearing that I recognized their moods and appeared to be in touch with my own. My parents based their accusations on what they thought they read on my face. Their assumptions were not always accurate. As a result, I tried to hide my feelings.

Burying Feelings Can Be Detrimental

Pushing aside your feelings and emotions may temporarily submerge them, but they are still very much alive and can resurface at the most inopportune times. Attempting to hide or deny our pain is not a helpful strategy. We need to open our hearts to the Lord and hand over our pain. The enemy loves to see us struggling with feelings of guilt, fear, and shame. Our Lord waits for us to give our feelings to Him so He can restore our hearts and share His truth.

Micah 7:18–19 describes God's steadfast love and acceptance and states God will have compassion for us and cast our sins into the depths of the sea. When we instead chose to hold onto painful memories, we allow guilt to manipulate us. We do not need to remain in self-imposed prisons of guilt, fear, and shame. The Lord wants to mend our broken hearts. He demonstrated this when He came to earth.

Press and I prayed for Paula, a woman in her eighties, one night after visiting friends while on vacation in 2016. When asked what she would like the Lord to heal, Paula immediately mentioned almost drowning when she was about eight or nine years old. She admitted she had talked about this experience many times and knew she was afraid to swim in the ocean and pools because of two near-drowning incidents.

She vehemently added this was in the past, so it should not be bothering her. She asserted it was a non-issue. Paula continued to defend her position that this should be a non-issue, even though we were not arguing or challenging her. She appeared to be trying to convince herself she should not focus on this painful memory. It seemed clear to us this was an upsetting recollection buried alive for almost seventy-five years.

Press explained these experiences, and the resulting emotions and feelings, are often buried alive. They stay submerged until they are brought to the surface for Jesus to repair. He asked her if she would like to invite Jesus into this memory. Paula agreed.

We asked the Lord to come into the prayer session. Paula closed her eyes and recalled the first near-drowning incident. She described in detail the events of that holiday outing. Her dad and uncle rented a small vessel and planned to spend the day boating in the East River with Paula and her older sister. They were excited about the opportunity.

Amid the excitement of the day, young Paula leaned over the boat to look for fish coming to the surface. She leaned over too far and fell into the river. Paula did not know how to swim and panicked, thrashing her arms wildly while she unsuccessfully tried to stay above the surface of the water. Her dad jumped into the water and rescued her. He then carried her soaking wet to their car in the adjacent parking lot. He placed her in the car, locked the doors, and went back to the boat to join the rest of the family.

Paula cried at this point in her story, saying she was put in the car all alone for the rest of the day because she ruined the family's outing. She said they had already paid for the boat and did not want to lose their money or the chance to spend the day on the river. Paula described herself sitting in the car, shaking in her wet clothes and frightened. Convinced this was punishment for spoiling the family outing, she sat there shivering all alone and felt banished and rejected.

Paula described what she saw in her mind's eye when she sat in the car that afternoon. She described the soft upholstery and the blanket she snuggled against in the back seat. Then she added, "Oh my goodness. I fell asleep. I did not realize that I slept most of that afternoon. In the past, when I replayed that day over in my mind, my heart pounded in my chest, and my body shook like when I shivered in my wet clothes. I saw myself abandoned, frightened, and panicked for many waking hours. I did not realize I must have slept all afternoon."

At this point, Paula's breathing visibly slowed and her hunched shoulders relaxed. She appeared comforted by learning that she calmly slept for most of that afternoon. Press invited Paula to look around the car and see if there was anyone with her. When she said that she could not see anyone with her, Press suggested she look down at the car from above. While continuing to focus on the memory with her eyes closed, she said she sensed Jesus's presence in the car soothing and consoling her. His company during this traumatic time was a new revelation for her. We were quiet while Paula rested for several moments in Jesus's comfort and the knowledge she was not alone in the car after all.

She then told us her dad relayed the afternoon boating events to her mother when they arrived home later that day. Paula's mother responded by yelling, saying that Paula ruined the day. She was sent to bed without dinner. Paula believed she deserved chastisement and was responsible for spoiling the family's day. Then Paula told us her mother accused her of ruining another holiday.

While outside by herself skating several months earlier, Paula fell and broke her arm. When she came into the house writhing in pain, holding her broken arm, her mother screamed, "How could you do this to me? How could you ruin my holiday?" While she relayed this story, Paula's face gave the impression she just realized something did not make sense. She was the one in pain trying to hold her arm limply hanging from her shoulder, and yet her mother claimed she was the one with the messed-up holiday.

We invited Paula to ask Jesus for the truth about these situations and her mother's reaction. He revealed that her mother reacted out of her woundedness and fear of what others might say and not because the little girl was an evil person, as she had believed for years. Jesus told her it was a lie that she spoiled the holidays and deserved punishment. She appeared grateful to learn the truth regarding the situation.

The most poignant part of the prayer time came after Paula was asked if she would like Jesus to take her to Father God. She quickly said, "Yes," and then described the glowing white light she saw surrounding Father God sitting high on a throne.

She said she must be in the throne room she heard about in church services. I thought this was a fantastic blessing and encounter for Paula. She told us Jesus held her hand and introduced her to God. At that point, she broke out in uncontrollable sobs, trembling as her body shook and rocked back and forth. This display of emotion was highly unusual for Paula, who previously told us she prided herself in guarding her feelings.

After several moments, we asked if she could share her encounter with us. She said in halting sobs that God stepped down off His high throne with His arms reaching out toward her. He came down to meet her and Jesus. She kept saying in an incredulous tone, "He came down to me. Why? Why would He do this? I don't deserve this. I am not worthy. Why?" She continued to reiterate that she was not worthy while turning her head to the side as if looking away from the vision. The Lord showed her she had believed a lie. She was, indeed, worthy.

I sensed Paula suffered from fear, shame, and unworthiness most of her life. We knew Paula for many years and were aware she remained isolated because of fear of being hurt by others and was reticent to take risks. We rarely saw her express emotions openly. She often commented the world was scary, and she vowed she would never let anyone hurt her again.

In the prayer session, the Lord showed her she did not need to fear. He was always with her, even in the traumatic events of her life. She visualized herself sitting on Father God's lap, basking in His unconditional love for several minutes. Paula's face streaming with tears of joy reflected the wonder of these profound, personal moments with God. She had heard many times in sermons how much God loves His children. But it was not until Paula experienced His love in this intimate encounter that she believed she was cherished by God.

Press asked Paula if she would like to seek God's forgiveness for believing the enemy's lies. She did ask for His forgiveness. She sensed Father God told her she was worthy because of Jesus and no longer needed to worry that she was not good enough. She understood her value was not based on what she did, but rather on what Jesus, who lives in her, did at the cross.

The enemy unfairly gained access through this traumatic event when Paula was vulnerable, causing her to fear and believe falsehoods about herself and her worth. She tried to bury these feelings of shame, guilt, and fear for over seven decades, not realizing she needed to release them to the Lord. He healed her pain and showed Paula aspects of the traumatic event she was unaware of once she asked Him. He can do the same for you.

Pray this prayer aloud:

> Lord, thank you for creating me with emotions designed to protect and motivate me. I repent for believing the lie that I am fatally flawed, which caused me to hide my feelings from others. You created me in Your image, and my identity is in You. Please forgive me for judging my feelings and consequently trying to bury them. Expose my feelings to Your light and reveal any areas in need of healing. Thank you, Lord. Amen.

Chapter 14

Guilt

We observed that feelings of guilt and shame frequently resulted from trauma people suffered early in life, similar to Paula's story. Sometimes others told them they needed to forget what happened and not dwell on the situation. Other times, either the person misinterpreted the events and believed they caused the suffering or someone else blamed them, and they accepted this accusation as truth.

Believing lies is often the case with young children who do not have the wisdom and experience to understand the circumstances in their lives fully. We met Adrian at the prison. He told us he stopped putting candles in church and praying for his brother when he was a child. Raised in the Russian Orthodox faith, he frequently saw people lighting candles, making an offering, and praying for loved ones. His family regularly lit candles and strongly encouraged him to light them for his brother's health. At age thirty-three, he still believed his brother died because he stopped burning candles at church for him. Mercifully, Jesus healed his heart and took his false guilt over this situation during prayer.

We repeatedly observed that traumatic events were buried and not dealt with until prayer recipients met the Lord in an inner healing prayer session. Then the Lord showed them aspects of the disturbing situation they were unaware of, similar to Paula's encounter with the Lord. When they gave their pain to the Lord, He showed them His love and restored their hearts. They realized they were trying to protect themselves and avoid further wounding when they instead needed to give the heartache to the Lord. Jesus wants us to live in peace.

In John 14:27, Jesus said, "Peace I leave with you; my peace I give to you. Not as the world gives do I give to you. Let not your hearts be troubled, neither let them be afraid." We will feel the Lord's peace when we invite Him into our hearts. When we recognize our identity is in Christ, we realize we carry His peace because we have Him inside us. When we have not understood our real identity, we can succumb to fear, guilt, and even physical illness. Jesus is the answer to all our problems.

Guilt plagues many people and results in considerable suffering and anguish. This emotional pain and wounding can also manifest as physical illness and wreak havoc in our bodies. We need to discern whether the guilt we feel is because of sinful behavior against God or the enemy's accusations.

False guilt or condemnation is from the devil, our accuser. We may believe the enemy's lies when we are not grounded in our identity in Christ. R. T. Kendall describes false guilt as a sense of shame we carry in our hearts that was not placed there by God.[2]

The Holy Spirit does not condemn but instead convicts us of sin. This conviction should lead us to repent and seek forgiveness for the sinful behavior that caused us to feel guilty. 1 John 1:9 says: "If we confess our sins, he is faithful and just to forgive us our sins and to cleanse us from all unrighteousness." We need to bring these feelings to the Lord for Him to speak His truth into our lives. If we are experiencing false guilt and condemnation, the Lord can tell us and show us how to walk in peace.

Unfortunately, many people hold onto guilt, both false and genuine guilt over their mistakes, never sharing this with anyone, which allows it to fester. False guilt and the associated shame robs people of the peace the Lord desires for their lives.

Press and I observed that false guilt often developed after people endured traumatic events and believed lies about themselves concerning the ordeal. We saw this pattern with the men we prayed for at the prison. A desire to rid themselves of guilt and shame led many to pray for peace to reign in their lives. The following five stories are typical of what we often heard.

Irwin, a man in his twenties, met with us for prayer one afternoon in 2018. He told us he could not rid himself of intense feelings of guilt over not adequately protecting his sister. We asked Irwin if he would like to invite Jesus to reveal the root of the belief that he was responsible for her behavior. He said yes, and with his eyes closed, he asked Jesus to show him when he first came to believe this lie.

In his mind's eye, Irwin saw his mother telling him at age six, several days after his dad abandoned the family, that he needed to be the man of the family and protect his sister. Jesus showed him it was not his responsibility to stop his sister from making poor choices. After Jesus told Irwin He did not give him this assignment, Irwin forgave his mother for those words spoken to him and his dad for leaving the family. He repented for living his life based on this false guilt. With tears in his eyes, he thanked Jesus for revealing the origin of his false guilt and taking away the pain associated with thinking his sister's behavior was his responsibility. He said Jesus filled him with calmness and peace. Our prayer was for him to continue to experience the Lord's peace.

Diego heard others in the prison talking about how Jesus healed their broken hearts and changed their lives. He requested healing prayer to ask the Lord to change his life and rid him of his long suffering. Diego wanted to start living a clean and moral life and give up his addiction to alcohol, which had led to his incarceration.

We asked Diego through our translator, Pablo, if he would like to invite Jesus into the memory where his hurt and guilt began. Diego agreed, closed his eyes, and asked Jesus to expose the root of his guilt.

Immediately, Diego saw himself in his mind's eye at age seven in his home with his mother. Diego's dad just moved out of their house, leaving his mom to raise their three sons alone. He described feeling overwhelmed and sad while he sat in the kitchen with his head face down on the table, wishing he could take back the last words he spoke to his dad before his abrupt departure. Diego sobbed when he recalled feeling entirely responsible for his dad's separation from the family. He could not lift his head from the table to look his mother in the eye because of the overwhelming weight of guilt he felt.

Press asked Diego if there was anyone else, besides his mother, with him in the kitchen. At that moment, Jesus showed Diego that He had been with him in the kitchen. Diego lifted his head, opened his eyes, and exclaimed, "I felt so alone and crushed with guilt, but I see I was not alone." Diego said he would like to give his false guilt to Jesus. He extended his arms upward and said, "Jesus, please take this guilt from me."

With a huge smile on his face, Diego told us Jesus lifted a huge burden off his shoulders and showed him that he had nothing to do with his dad's leaving. Pablo asked Diego if he would like to receive Jesus as his Lord and Savior. "Yes," Diego cried out. Pablo led Diego in a prayer to receive Jesus. Diego accepted Jesus as his Lord and Savior and received the Lord's peace and healing of his broken heart.

Mario, a young man in his mid-twenties in the prison, sobbed when he shared his life story and need for a touch from the Lord. He accepted Jesus as his Lord and Savior one month before we met him for prayer. Mario asked Jesus to forgive him for his bad choices and grant him a long life.

At age five, his parents divorced after much quarreling. Mario claimed his mother's family openly expressed anger toward him and shunned him because he looked like his estranged father. Insufficient funds were a constant issue in the family and caused numerous arguments and fighting.

Mario's shoulders and hands shook while tears streamed down his face when he told us his grandfather sent him to the dump to get food during a fight with his mother over lack of money. He could not remember ever experiencing peace at home—only rejection in his chaotic family. Mario stopped attending school and left home in his early teens to live with a young girl.

Mario and his girlfriend soon started a family of their own and had two daughters. They brought their first daughter to the emergency room at two months of age because she had difficulty breathing. The young infant gasped for breath and her lips turned blue, which frightened both parents. Several seconds passed before she could catch her breath again. Then the gasping and wheezing returned. The doctors admitted her to the hospital that evening for observation and further testing to diagnose the respiratory problem. She died several days later after contracting an illness while being treated in the medical facility.

Their second daughter died during childbirth after a staff member broke her shoulder while assisting with the problematic delivery. The midwife was unable to resuscitate her. Out of anguish, Mario's girlfriend blamed his drug use for their children's deaths when they returned home. Obscenities flew out of her mouth, and she hurled furniture, threatening to leave him. The next day he awoke to find her and her belongings gone.

To ease the guilt weighing on him after his girlfriend left prior to his eighteenth birthday, Mario turned again to alcohol and drugs. Alone and abandoned, he sought companionship with others who promised him loyalty. This allegiance came with a price—gang membership. Shortly after his initiation, he committed crimes he never thought he would do. If he did not obey the demands from the gang leaders, he faced their punishment in the form of physical harm and possible death. If he followed their orders, he risked police arrest if caught. A year later, he escaped from the gang but was apprehended by the police and incarcerated.

When we met Mario, he said he desperately wanted a fresh start. He did not want his new wife and child to suffer any repercussions from his previous choices. He wanted to be free of the constant thoughts in his mind telling him he was worthless and to blame for his children's deaths and failed marriage.

Mario gave his false guilt and grief over his daughters' deaths to Jesus during our prayer time. He repented for his subsequent bad choices, involving addiction and gang involvement, and the genuine guilt he felt over those behaviors. Mario also broke several negative generational influences over his life and his future generations. He specifically prayed for the Lord to protect his new wife and infant son.

Mario broke unhealthy connections with several women, family members, and gang partners and asked the Lord to bless them. His face reflected the release and freedom he found in Christ. We referred him to the prison chaplain to guide him in his new relationship with Jesus.

Childhood memories silently tormented Jorge until he brought them to the light for Jesus to take. He was nine years old when he and his sister were left alone to care for their baby brother. Jorge and his sister successfully escaped their home when flames engulfed the house. But their baby brother perished in the fire, and his parents blamed Jorge. He carried this false guilt and responsibility for years. Later, his parents blamed him for another brother's murder, despite Jorge having no way to prevent this deadly attack.

Jorge appeared to be the family's scapegoat, and he accepted this role. The family sought help by going to magicians and witch doctors, which only exacerbated their problems. Jorge felt Jesus had abandoned him, so he also sought protection from a witch doctor by paying him thousands of dollars.

Then, four months before we met Jorge, he rededicated his life to Jesus and asked for forgiveness. He wanted to start his life over on the right path this time. When we joined Jorge in prayer, he broke ancestral influences associated with the occult, addiction, fear, victimization, and sexual abuse. After he felt oppression lift off him, he shared another traumatic event he silently concealed for twenty years.

The Lord healed this buried memory and took his guilt, fear, and shame. Jorge left the session, convinced the Lord forgave him and believing there is no condemnation for those in Christ Jesus. He indeed was a new creation. Jorge told us that he had joined the men's Bible study in his unit and planned to share his testimony. If the Lord could help him, he wanted others to know that Jesus would help them too.

Ricardo felt sadness, remorse, and guilt over his eighteen-year-old sister's death in 2008. She was two years younger than him and had been sick most of her life. In 2006, she had a kidney transplant. Her health slowly started to improve after the long surgical recovery. Although she struggled with fatigue, she started showing interest in family parties and gatherings again. Her family hoped this was a sign that she would finally enjoy a normal life. On Easter Sunday morning, Ricardo convinced his sister to go to church with him. He promised to take her out to lunch after the service. At first, she wanted to stay in bed and rest, but the promise of going to a restaurant enticed her. She got out of bed to shower and get ready for the afternoon outing. While in the shower, she slipped, fell, and hit her head on the tile floor. The family rushed her to the hospital. She died shortly after the fall, most likely because of bleeding in her brain.

Ricardo's family was left devasted. Each person retreated inwardly in an attempt to deal with their unbearable sorrow. They did not share their pain. Instead, they each tried to bury their heartache. Ricardo's mother turned to prescription drugs. His dad worked long hours and rarely was home. Ricardo bore the responsibility for her death and, as a result, turned to alcohol and other addictive behaviors, which led to estrangement from the family. Several years later, he turned his life back over to the Lord when in prison.

Ricardo told us he was now aware of God's grace and hand in his life. He said he knew the Lord forgave him when he earnestly asked. Ricardo currently teaches and preaches to other incarcerated men. He particularly loves the stories of Joseph and Job and how God turned their tragedies around and provided them with more than they could ever have imagined. The Lord can do the same for you today. Ask Him. He stands at the door, waiting for you to invite Him in.

Pray this prayer aloud:

> Lord, I give You the heavy burden of false guilt I have been carrying. You said in the Bible that that Your yoke is easy and Your burden is light. Yet, I continued to take responsibility for people and situations that were not mine to take. Please help me discern true guilt that needs repentance from false guilt, which is a ploy of the enemy. I understand the Holy Spirit convicts us of the truth, but the enemy condemns us. Help me rely on Your Holy Spirit for the truth. Amen.

CHAPTER 15

Fear

Fear, often the result of upsetting life events, led numerous people in our community and the prison ministry to request healing prayer. They asked the Lord to take away the terror and paralyzing fear they were suffering.

Several men we prayed with through the prison ministry witnessed the murder of family members and friends. Some of the slayings they saw occurred when they were young. They fled the scene in fear for their safety, resulting in false guilt over not helping their loved ones during the attack. Continual panic and anxiety overwhelmed them in their adult years. During prayer, the Lord showed them they were not responsible for the deaths, and He released their fear. We prayed they would continue to experience the Lord's peace.

Some men described victimization by gang members and others by family members. They fled their countries to escape being hunted down by gang members because of what they witnessed. During prayer, Jesus showed several men how He saved their lives and protected them when attacked. Others felt relief when they sensed the Lord completely forgave them. They no longer needed to be afraid after Jesus showed them that they believed in a lie about the situation and themselves. They renounced the falsehood and accepted the Lord's forgiveness and truth.

One of the men we prayed with, Joaquin, described himself as a victim because he frequently seemed to be in the wrong place at the wrong time. He experienced abuse during his childhood, which led him to feel worthless and abandoned. Gangs repeatedly tried to coerce him into membership. The more he resisted their forceful attempts, the more they physically intimidated him and threatened to take his life.

He described a frightening and disturbing occurrence when a gang member shoved a gun into his mouth and then wielded a machete in front of him, motioning how it would cut him into pieces if he did not comply with their demands. His mother feared for his life and sent him to an occult practitioner who promised to provide a safe house. The empty promises and requests for more money from this consultant increased his fear and reinforced Joaquin's view of himself as a victim.

Joaquin came to the United States seeking safety. Fleeing his country did not provide the security and freedom from fear that he sought. Anxiety, oppression, and nightmares continued to afflict him. He did not maintain steady employment and lacked money for daily necessities, which led him to associate with others who took advantage of him. We explained the concept of generational curses and the importance of breaking these negative influences. Joaquin said he wanted these influences to stop affecting him. We guided him through prayers to break the ancestral impacts of victimization, abuse and trauma, fear, addiction, poverty, death, and the occult. Joaquin forgave the people who hurt him and broke ungodly soul ties. He realized his only absolute safety is in the Lord. He repeatedly thanked Jesus for releasing his fear.

The incarcerated men who requested asylum from war-torn countries told some of the more heart-wrenching stories. Charles, a professional photographer, sought asylum from a war-torn country after military separatists abducted him and attempted to kill him. They accused him of taking photos for the opposition at an event. Although Charles claimed the event was not associated with the military or government, they still followed him home and abducted him. Charles was taken to a cell and beaten and tortured until a lawyer arranged for his release.

His family worried about his safety, so they insisted he hide in the jungle. He remained concealed in the bush for over four months, surviving on little food, and became ill. While in hiding, Charles received word that the military shot his cousin in front of his wife and children. The soldiers mistakenly thought they had killed Charles.

Persistent fear for his life and guilt over his cousin's death tormented Charles. His mother helped arrange for him to come to the United States to seek asylum. His arduous journey took many months, passing through several countries, making his way thousands of miles to the United States. He had a vision of Jesus meeting him in the jungle during healing prayer, telling him he was not to blame for his cousin's death. He then described how Jesus took him to meet Father God. After Charles asked the Lord to take the trauma and fear he endured, he felt the Lord release his burdens, and he experienced freedom. We found out several weeks later that he also received asylum and looked forward to his new life of freedom.

Henry resided in the United States for the past sixteen years and desperately wanted to remain in the United States. When living overseas, he witnessed his dad's death at age five and was captured by rebels and taken from his family to be a soldier at age ten. The rebels threatened to kill him and his family if he did not follow their orders and commit crimes against others.

Although Henry escaped the rebels after one month of captivity, feelings of guilt and fear plagued him daily. He said he continued to suffer from Post Traumatic Distress Disorder and indicated medication did not alleviate his symptoms and tormenting thoughts. Henry feared God was mad at him because he followed rebel orders while in captivity. He stated that he asks the Lord every day for forgiveness and peace.

Henry said he previously prayed with several highly regarded pastors. These clergy tried to help him get over or through the thick, black wall he described sensing when encountering the Lord during prayer. He said some pastors wanted him to envision allowing them to climb from the other side to pull him over the wall, but this was not a successful strategy. Tormenting thoughts continued to plague him.

When we prayed with Henry, he broke generational influences associated with murder and death, violence, anger, trauma, condemnation, and the occult. Henry also broke unhealthy soul ties and forgave the rebels and the men who killed his dad. Although Henry appeared to receive some freedom, we sensed more prayer was needed to focus on removing any remaining occult influences from his involvement with voodoo. Unfortunately, we did not have the opportunity to meet with him again. We prayed that he would continue to seek the Lord and experience redemption from the God who never gives up on His children.

In 2 Timothy 1:7, we are reminded God did not give us a spirit of fear but one "of power and love and self-control." Yet, many who identify as Christians experience tremendous fear and anxiety, even if they have not endured incarceration or witnessed a horrific event. Fear will attempt to thwart our God-given destiny. It can keep us locked in an emotional prison even if we never experience imprisonment in a jail cell. Despite intellectually knowing Jesus is our hope and peace, many people remain bound in a state of alarm because their hearts have not fully embraced the truth in 2 Timothy 1:7. I was one of those people for many years.

I spent a significant amount of time striving, performing, and believing I could figure out how to achieve peace if I just tried hard enough. I did not realize I needed to understand God's heart for me and believe I was His valued daughter. I did not need to keep trying to seek the Lord's acceptance because I already had it. His approval was not based on what I did but on my identity in Him as His beloved child.

I acted as a slave rather than a valued daughter of the Lord of the universe—my true identity. I viewed God as a master instead of as a loving father. Leif Hetland, the founder of Global Mission Awareness, describes this as having an orphan spirit. Hetland stated only Father God's perfect love displaces fear.[3]

We come against fear by daily putting on the full armor of God that Paul referred to in Ephesians 6. This spiritual armor includes the belt of truth, breastplate of righteousness, shoes of the gospel of peace, the shield of faith, the helmet of salvation, and the sword of the Spirit, which is God's Word. Paul reminds us that we do not wrestle against others but instead against spiritual forces of evil. We need to pray persistently to the Lord.

Paul also acknowledges that we will face trials and tribulations, but we have access to our Lord, who is our help. He will never forsake us. In 2 Corinthians 4:8–10, Paul writes,

"We are afflicted in every way, but not crushed; perplexed, but not driven to despair; persecuted, but not forsaken; struck down, but not destroyed; always carrying in the body the death of Jesus, so that the life of Jesus may also be manifested in our bodies."

Pray this prayer aloud:

> Lord, please forgive me for partnering with the spirit of fear and associated feelings of shame and unworthiness, and allowing them to wreak havoc in my life. Lord, in place of the fear I allowed in my life, I ask for Your peace to reign in me. I stand on Your Word in Psalm 62 that says You are my rock, my salvation, and my fortress, and I shall not be shaken. Amen.

CHAPTER 16

Redemption through Emotional Healing

Our God is a God of many chances and is in the business of redemption. In Ephesians 1:7, Paul speaks of Jesus and writes, "In him we have redemption through his blood, the forgiveness of our trespasses, according to the riches of his grace."

Numerous verses in the Old Testament also point to the Lord as our redeemer. Even though Job's life was falling apart, he declared with authority in Job 19:25, "For I know that my Redeemer lives, and at the last he will stand upon the earth." Isaiah, the prophet, assured Israel that God had not forgotten them when he recorded in Isaiah 44:22, "I have blotted out your transgressions like a cloud and your sins like mist; return to me, for I have redeemed you."

When we first met Adriano in the prison, he enthusiastically told us God intervened and prevented a deportation order to Central America. Adriano spent the majority of his adult years incarcerated. Despite accepting Jesus as his Savior twenty-two years earlier, Adriano admitted making bad choices and living his life apart from the Lord. Adriano acknowledged that he had not always been honest. He claimed he could now see God's hand in his life and was thankful for another chance to join his family and remain in the United States. Adriano sincerely wanted to get his life right with the Lord. He emphatically declared he was ready to accept full responsibility for his actions. We had not met with anyone so enthusiastic for a new beginning.

As a teenager, Adriano lived with guilt and shame and accepted the lie that he was the family's designated black sheep. Just as happens with self-fulfilling prophecies, Adriano lived his life as if this assigned role was real. He and his friend were victims of a drive-by shooting at age sixteen. Adriano survived, but his friend did not. Adriano blamed himself for not saving his friend in time and sought to hurt the person who killed his friend and wounded him. His guilt over his friend's death, coupled with his anger and desire for revenge, led to poor choices and a subsequent arrest.

Adriano's suffering intensified at age eighteen when his father, Miguel, died on Adriano's parole day. Adriano told us several times that losing Miguel wounded him deeply and left a hole in his heart. Adriano's plans to reunite with Miguel would never be realized. Miguel considered Adriano his favorite child and now Adriano's number one cheerleader was gone. Increased self-condemnation led to a failed suicide attempt and unsuccessful pleas to others to end his life.

Adriano spent all but three of the following twenty-four years in prison suffering loss and trauma. He was left alone in his cell to grieve when several family members died. He endured numerous physical altercations and orchestrated attacks on other gang members, which led to frequent placements in isolation.

After we explained the concept of forgiveness, Adriano said he was at last ready to let go of his emotional pain and release his offenders. He desired the Lord's peace and understood forgiveness would bring freedom. We guided Adriano to forgive the people who assaulted him, physically and verbally. He broke generational influences associated with addiction, death, suicide, anger, revenge, aggression, victimization, trauma, sexual immorality, and the occult. Adriano asked the Lord to forgive him for partnering with these negative patterns. Additionally, Adriano broke the lie that he was the black sheep in his family.

When we met Adriano one month later, he excitedly told us he received baptism by immersion. He indicated he now realized life was no longer just about him. He also sought to stop domestic violence in his family. Adriano was encouraged when his son shared over the phone that he was breaking the pattern of domestic abuse in his young family.

Adriano indicated his three adult children now trusted him enough to share significant issues and seek his input. He was anxious to be reunited with his family because he believed they needed him. As we prayed and blessed Adriano, I sensed the Lord wanted him to know perfection was not the expectation.

Although Adriano will likely face some disappointments and challenges when he navigates life outside of prison, he will not be back at square one again. Adriano knows Jesus will take all his fears and temptations and give him a fresh start. All he needs to do is continue to release them to the Lord and ask for forgiveness and direction.

During our final meeting with Adriano, we were surprised to learn he had been reading Christian books on emotional wholeness. He identified more negative family patterns that needed breaking, and he fervently prayed for release from oppression. He excitedly showed us one of the books he received from the library. We immediately recognized the Stormie Omartian book, *Prayers for Emotional Wholeness*, that once sat on the bookshelf in our friend Madeline's home.

Madeline was a prayer warrior in our church who died because of cancer, and her son had donated her books to the prison library. We were thrilled to see her legacy carried on. Adriano told us he faithfully prayed the book's prayers to release bound emotions. He told us he was scheduled for release from prison soon and asked us to pray with him that day to break depression, fear, doubt, and expectations of failure.

Adriano reiterated stories of how God saved his life numerous times. He recalled a time in Mexico when left for dead bleeding, and the Lord miraculously spared his life. Adriano emphatically declared that the Lord allowed his previous release from jail. When he looked to a church to mentor him after that release, they could not help him. Adriano promised to seek a Christian church to disciple him after he leaves prison. He was determined not to let the disappointment over the previous church's failure to provide guidance deter him this time.

Convinced God has a purpose for his life, Adriano was excited to start his new life by reconnecting with his family. He wanted to be the dad he could not be to his children while incarcerated. When we prayed for the Lord to send him people who could walk beside him and shepherd him, I sensed the Lord wanted him to know that he would be an ambassador.

Freedom from Distressing Emotions

Almost all of the people we prayed with received relief from the Lord for the distressing emotions plaguing them. However, inner healing is a process that often occurs in stages or layers, similar to the way we peel an onion layer by layer. Although the Lord can instantly restore a person, we frequently observed that healing occurred in stages for most people.

We were blessed to meet with a few men like Adriano on more than one occasion through the prison ministry and see their healing progression. Typically, we were only able to meet with those men one time. Our closing prayer included asking the Lord to send mentors and people to disciple them in their Christian walk. Most of the men who requested healing prayer professed to be Christians. Some men had turned away from the Lord. A few men heard about Jesus but had not previously committed to following Him. Several men rededicated their lives to Jesus when we met with them, and a few accepted Jesus as their Lord and Savior when we prayed together. Seeing their transformation while they received the Lord and revealed what Jesus showed them brought us great joy.

When we prayed with people, we often asked, "What would you like the Lord to heal for you today?" A typical response from the men who lived through incarceration was "I want the Lord to forgive me and heal me." Several men sought asylum from war-scarred countries. They wanted the Lord to intervene to prevent deportation to these countries where they risked death upon their return. Occasionally, the men asked for physical healing, but most requests were for emotional and spiritual healing.

Many men wanted to be free from emotions and feelings that seemed to paralyze them and lock them in fear, guilt, and shame. Their prayer requests were not much different from those we prayed with who had not experienced incarceration or intense trauma. Most people wanted to feel the Lord's peace and receive a release from distressing emotions such as shame, guilt, unworthiness, condemnation, fear, anxiety, and depression. They wanted assurance of the Lord's forgiveness and frequently asked for His direction in their life.

We often heard the following requests from the men who faced incarceration:

I want the Lord to

- heal my shame
- heal my heart and mind and forgive me
- heal depression, fear, doubt, and expectations of failure
- change my character so that I walk in obedience
- give me peace and release
- give me a sense of belonging
- give me freedom from addiction
- help me know my purpose
- give me wisdom, understanding, and protection
- show me how I can serve Jesus
- stop domestic violence in my family

During prayer, the Lord often uncovered the root of the negative emotions and the resulting lies the men believed. When they forgave the people who hurt them and asked God to forgive them for their part in accepting the lies and their resulting actions, He healed their suffering. Their emotional pain no longer imprisoned them. We observed the same freedom and release from distressing feelings for people who never experienced physical imprisonment but were held in bondage by emotional wounds. Jesus indeed came to set the captives free.

Pray this prayer aloud:

> Lord, thank you that You never gave up on me. You truly are the God of many chances. Jesus died to set me free from my fears and sins. I now accept His forgiveness that makes me a new creation. I am free of negative emotions, including guilt, fear, shame, and condemnation. I know I am loved and redeemed. Amen.

CHAPTER 17

Visual Healing Encounters

Afterprayer recipients broke negative generational influences and
unhealthy soul ties during their prayer sessions, they often asked the
Lord for relief from their emotional distress. The Lord met each person in
a way that was uniquely meaningful to them, and He healed their broken
hearts. Sometimes the person visually recalled a painful memory.

Other times they envisioned the Lord meeting them in a special place.
Press and I were careful to wait on the Lord to see what He would do when
the prayer recipients closed their eyes and invited Him into their hearts.

We met Martin through the prison ministry. He came to the United
States twelve years earlier after gang members killed his brother and
attempted to kill him in Central America. We led him in prayers to break
unhealthy soul ties and generational curses associated with violence, death,
trauma, abandonment, addiction, and sexual sin.

When Martin asked the Lord to heal his traumatic memory, he pictured
himself in a river on a bright sunny day and felt the Lord wash his sins away.
His facial expression evidenced the joy and peace he experienced as Jesus
took his sins and cleansed him. I thought the Lord called Martin a *conqueror*

and *his man on the ground* and shared this with him. Immediately, Martin clapped his hands and repeated, "Yes, yes."

He explained that the chaplain baptized him a few weeks earlier, and now he taught others about Jesus by leading a men's Bible study. He believed the Lord saved his life for a reason, and he wanted to fulfill his God-given destiny.

When we met Lorenzo at the prison, he said he wanted God to give him peace and guide his life in the right direction. Lorenzo grew up in a war-torn country in Central America and witnessed his dad's murder in 2000 when he was fifteen years old. Subsequent physical altercations with his older brother led Lorenzo to disengage from the family. He indicated he experienced guilt and shame over not spending more time with his sisters since leaving the family. Lorenzo also grieved the loss of his nine-year-old daughter, who died because of a throat illness. The loss and trauma he endured left him devastated.

During prayer, Lorenzo broke the family's negative generational patterns associated with spirits of violence, death, trauma, abandonment, victimization, addiction, and sexual sin. He forgave his ancestors and asked the Lord to forgive him for any part he played in these negative patterns. Lorenzo sensed the Lord blessed him with peace and acceptance as a beloved son. Lorenzo said he wanted to invite the Lord to heal his heart from the shock and loss he sustained in his family and war-torn country.

Lorenzo closed his eyes and, in a soft voice, asked the Lord to mend his heart. His rapid speech slowed down as he smiled, and the tense muscles in his arms and hands visibly relaxed. Several moments passed while we observed Lorenzo quietly interacting with the Lord. His demeanor reflected a peace we had not seen earlier when he shared his life story. After Lorenzo opened his eyes, he told us that he sensed meeting the Holy Spirit and Jesus in a river. Lorenzo said he saw a bird flying around his neck when he asked Jesus to heal his trauma. He did receive the peace and freedom he earnestly requested.

We observed that feelings of guilt, shame, and fear often occurred simultaneously in the people requesting prayer. Costanzo rededicated his life to the Lord several months before we met him in the prison. His current prayer request was for the Holy Spirit to redirect his life. He wanted to be free of the shameful memories he carried. When Costanzo was four years old, he shaved his head to look bald like his dad. This left scars on his scalp. When questioned by his parents, he said his seven-year-old brother shaved his head.

As a result, his brother was punished and forced to work to pay the associated medical expenses. At age ten, Costanzo told his parents the truth regarding the incident and did not receive punishment for lying. He asked the Lord for forgiveness. Still, Costanzo felt guilt and shame and wanted to ask his brother to forgive him for falsely blaming him almost thirty-eight years earlier.

Costanzo described another traumatic incident when he witnessed men fighting with machetes while living in Central America. The attackers, fearful Costanzo could identify them, followed him, shouting threats and punching him. He still carried fear, guilt, and shame from that event.

We invited him to ask the Lord, "Jesus, what am I still holding on to that you want me to release to You?" Costanzo believed he needed to break generational patterns in his lineage and ask for forgiveness for allowing these patterns to impact his life. He broke generational curses associated with shame, guilt, trauma, fear, unworthiness, sexual sin, and the occult.

Costanzo said the Lord gave him a vision. He described himself standing in a river, and a bright light shone on him. Costanzo felt a warm sense of peace and basked in this tranquility for several moments. He appeared overjoyed in the presence of the Lord. Costanzo left the prayer session with a lightness in his step after meeting the Lord and releasing his distressing emotions.

Shelia sought prayer to gain a deeper understanding of what the Lord desired for her. Since childhood, she had been aware of the Lord's voice in her life. He often spoke to her through dreams, thoughts, and visions. During prayer, Shelia broke several generational influences, including fear, trauma, and shame, which she believed led to bound emotions. She also broke several ungodly soul ties and word curses spoken over her.

With closed eyes, she asked the Lord to meet with her. Sheila appeared radiant, and her smile broadened when she saw the Lord in her mind's eye.

Sheila told us Jesus met her on a mountain top—her favorite landscape. Jesus told her that He was in her heart and was enamored with her. He reminded her of the words in Jeremiah 29:11, which read, "For I know the plans I have for you, declares the Lord, plans for welfare and not for evil, to give you a future and a hope."

Sheila asked Jesus to explain what He expected of her. She sensed He wanted her to be honest about her feelings and not try to bury or deny them as she had done in the past. He said many new things would be coming into her life, but this required letting go of the old stuff. Jesus introduced her to Father God, who said she no longer needed to strive to be good enough. She just needed to know Him.

At the end of the prayer session, Shelia excitedly told us of her plans to bask in God's presence at sunrise several mornings a week while overlooking the mountains near her home. She wanted to draw nearer to the Lord and enjoy His uninterrupted company in the quiet of the morning. I shared a vision of lots of manna from Heaven falling on Sheila while she was praying. We were excited to see what the Lord would do in Shelia's life when she drew closer to Him.

Lena requested a prayer appointment after seeing the change in others following their prayer sessions. She asked the Lord to show her what she needed to release to live in peace. The Lord exposed the unforgiveness that Lena still harbored toward her parents. After confessing this unforgiveness, Lena forgave her parents.

She enthusiastically shared that she frequently heard from the Lord through visions and pictures in her mind. As we prayed, Jesus showed her chinks in her spiritual armor that needed repair, specifically her helmet and breastplate. Lena thanked the Lord for her salvation and received it in a new fresh way, declaring nothing could separate her from the love of Christ. She vowed to wear Christ's righteousness against all condemnation and accept His protection from all assaults against her heart.

The second time we met with Lena, she asked Jesus to heal her heart. She imagined Jesus taking her to a meadow, playing and laughing with her when she was a young girl. He then showed her a black wind that came sweeping by bringing bitterness, hate, and resentment. The scene changed, and she saw herself as an adult experiencing vibrant colors in the meadow with Jesus. She believed the Lord wants her to rest in Him and completely forgive herself for past mistakes so she can be free again, laughing and playing with Him in the meadow and enjoying nature's brilliant colors.

Each prayer session we facilitated was different, just as every individual is unique. Not everyone meets the Lord through visions. I did not think I was a very visual person. When I drew closer to the Lord, I experienced Him more in visions and dreams. Some people sense the Lord's presence by thoughts in their minds. The Lord met each prayer recipient in a manner that was explicitly meaningful for them. He will do the same for you. He will meet you where you are. Invite Him into your heart.

Pray this prayer aloud:

> Thank you, Lord, that You are the God of many chances and are in the business of redemption. I thank you for redeeming me and healing my heart. Lord, please transform my mind and help me see people and situations the way You see them. Lord, I give You the negative feelings that are not from You and ask You to take them. In their place, I receive Your blessings of peace and healing. Help me put on Your full armor to stand against the enemy daily, as it says in Ephesians. Thank you for never forsaking me. I ask for Your continued guidance and presence through dreams, visions, and thoughts that You place in my mind. Amen.

SECTION 6

God is in Control

When we believe we have been abandoned and need to fend for ourselves, we attempt to orchestrate our lives. We may receive positive reinforcement for this lifestyle from others who believe the only way to live is to be self-reliant and independent. We may even profess to be Christians, but we do not live with God first in our minds. Because we mistakenly believe we are choreographing our lives, we do not turn to God for direction. In effect, we leave God out of our lives or put Him on the back burner when we hold on to this mindset. We may even identify with Simon and Garfunkel's song from the mid-1960s, "I Am a Rock,"[1] in an attempt to live as if we are a self-contained island to avoid pain.

CHAPTER 18

You Are Not Alone

I am not in control, but the Lord who loves me is in control. Unfortunately, I did not fully realize this until well into my adult years. Twila Paris tells us in her song, "God is in Control," that God holds the world together, so we have no reason to fear.[2] She reminds us that God continually watches over us and will never leave us.

Finally, after all this time, I gave up control. At least I thought I did. It can be challenging to surrender when you have managed your life for years. Or at least you thought you were choreographing your life.

Relinquishing control is particularly difficult when you have received positive reinforcement from others for your life management skills. For me, the desire to be in charge of my life began young. I received praise from elementary school teachers for my good grades. Their words spurred me to study diligently to gain their approval. Later, bosses and those in authority over me inspired my strong work ethic with favorable evaluations. These encouraging words led to my increased persistence and successful completion of tasks. From a worldly perspective, I demonstrated success. The work performance reviews and continued high grades through graduate school led me to believe I was doing all of the hard work independently. I erroneously thought I was in charge of my life.

Sadly, when we receive accolades for our self-sufficiency and self-reliance from those who share this worldview, we can believe we accomplished everything by our efforts. This is not God's intention for us. He designed us to be in a relationship with Him and depend on Him. We are to give Him complete control of our lives. We must release our lives entirely to the Lord to experience total freedom. It is the only option we have to live in peace and joy. In 1 Peter 5:7 we read to cast all our cares on the Lord because He cares for us.

Growing up, I learned from my parents it was necessary to "pull yourself up by your bootstraps" because you could only count on yourself. If something needed to get done, I believed I needed to do it myself to guarantee correct completion. I finished assignments at school, work, and home to the best of my ability and repeatedly placed a lot of pressure on myself, expecting perfection. This driven attitude transferred to my parenting skills.

As a young parent, I erroneously thought it was my responsibility to craft my children's environment to ensure they were always happy. I worked tirelessly to try to be the perfect parent while simultaneously working part-time or attending graduate school. I did not lean on God for His direction and wisdom, and I was not the ideal parent despite my diligent efforts. I served in church, but I had not fully grasped the reality that I did not need to figure out how to be the best parent, wife, employee, or student on my own. I had a loving God, a friend in Jesus, and a comforter and guide in the Holy Spirit who would navigate life for me if I would just let go and give Them the reins.

Although unaware at the time, I was, in effect, operating in what Leif Hetland calls the orphan spirit. Chester and Betsy Kylstra, founders of Restoring the Foundations (RTF), refer to this as the orphan lifestyle or orphan heart. The Kylstras contend this is not a spirit but rather a belief system, an attitude of our mind and heart. It is a lie of the enemy that convinces us we lack something and will do whatever is needed to protect ourselves.[3] Unfortunately, many people live their lives based on this false belief.

The Orphan Lifestyle

You can have parents and still live as though you are an orphan when you believe the lies that you are all alone, no one cares about you, and it is up to you to survive in the world. We prayed with many people who had parents and nevertheless felt alone or neglected. A spirit of abandonment—an underpinning of the orphan lifestyle—passes down through the family generations until we stop it through confession, repentance, and forgiveness.

Press and I did not realize this spirit was working in our family lines until we learned about healing prayer. We both wished we were aware of this earlier when we raised our children so these negative influences could have broken off our lineage then, not impacting our children. If we had been conscious of this when they were children, we could have exercised our authority as their parents to break these unhealthy patterns off them.

When we learned about generational curses, including the spirit of abandonment, we prayed to cut them off our family and future generations. We continue to pray daily for our children and grandchildren. Our children are now adults, and they need to break any negative influences impacting them. Our prayer is for them to recognize this and remove any adverse effects and generational curses off their children and future generations. Our parents and grandparents were unaware of generational influences and were negatively impacted by the spirit of abandonment.

My father experienced abandonment at age ten when his mother died. He and his sister came home from school to find her motionless in bed. Panicked, they called for help to rush her to the hospital. She never returned home again.

Family members told the children their mother died because of walking pneumonia in both lungs. No one was aware there was a bacterial infection silently raging in her lungs until she collapsed. I knew my grandmother died when my dad was ten, but I was not aware of the circumstances surrounding her death until my adult years. When I heard they found her unresponsive, I could not imagine the devastation and sense of helplessness and confusion my ten-year-old dad and his eleven-year-old sister must have felt.

My heart ached every time I imagined them coming home from school to find their mother unconscious and not understanding she would never return. My aunt went to live with an aunt and uncle, while my dad and grandfather lived with various relatives over the next several years. Relatives tired of my dad's misbehavior and requested that he and his father leave and relocate to live with other family members.

My dad then joined the Navy at age seventeen and was sent overseas to fight during World War II. After being wounded and receiving medical treatment overseas, he returned home at age nineteen and married his seventeen-year-old girlfriend. He believed marriage would provide stability and the sense of belonging he desired. My father had been searching for what he sensed he lacked—namely, a home, a place of belonging, a sense of peace, and a place of safety. These are characteristics of an orphan heart or an orphan lifestyle.

Problems soon arose in the marriage. Dad told me he shared his concerns regarding the difficulties in his young marriage with his father, hoping for advice and support. His father responded, "Son, you've made your bed. Now lie in it." Not the reaction he hoped to receive. Feelings of abandonment and rejection overwhelmed him.

I was surprised to learn that my father-in-law, Jerry, also experienced physical and emotional abandonment as a child and teen. I knew his father left when he was a toddler, leaving his mother to raise him and his two sisters. While we waited at the airport for Press to return from a business trip one evening, Jerry told me about some painful memories he had never shared with his children.

Jerry said his secretary had to leave work early that day because her eleven-year-old son's school announced an unexpected early dismissal. She did not want her son to be home alone, so she asked to leave work on short notice. That reminded Jerry he had been left alone as a young child and early teen. He told me his mother sent him and his sister to a Catholic boarding school during their elementary school years. They were not Catholic and felt somewhat out of place. During the summer months, his sister was allowed to go home and live with their mother, but he had to stay at the boarding school alone doing chores for the nuns while the other children also went home. He still seemed bewildered as to why his sister could go home and he could not.

Jerry continued to explain that while on vacation the previous summer with cousins, he visited the boarding school he lived at fifty years earlier. It was no longer functioning as a boarding facility, but he could visualize it precisely as it looked five decades ago while they walked the campus grounds. Jerry could see himself in the former storage building, tirelessly shoveling coal for the nuns.

His stomach churned and overwhelming nausea caught him off guard when he passed his former dormitory. Jerry never complained of physical ailments and was rarely sick, so this reaction stunned him. He explained the relentless, stabbing pain he felt in his gut as memories of those summer days alone working at the nuns' boarding school flooded back. I had known my father-in-law for twenty years at that time, and he had never shared childhood memories.

Although his children were curious about his bomber pilot experiences during World War II, he never talked about those either. We all assumed these memories must be too painful to discuss.

Press's plane was delayed, which gave us more time to talk together. Jerry then told me he used to help out at Uncle Press's ranch during his early teen years. As a tall and slim teen, Jerry was agile and worked hard many hours each day as a ranch hand, which pleased his uncle. Reflecting on this, he realized he did this to achieve recognition and identity. His aunt and uncle moved into town during the winter months when Jerry was fourteen, and they asked him to manage the ranch in their absence. He was thrilled his diligent work paid off and gained his uncle's recognition. Jerry stayed out on the Oklahoma ranch alone during the cold winter months overseeing the animals. His uncle came out every two weeks to make sure he had food.

Jerry said it never occurred to him at the time that this was unusual or today would not be considered a safe arrangement for a young teen. He described the pain he experienced in his gut associated with feeling incredibly lonely and isolated all winter on the ranch. As much as Jerry liked being needed and valued by his uncle, feelings of deep sadness and abandonment overwhelmed him. He said he coaxed the outside cat indoors to keep him company on the long winter nights. Her new litter soon joined them, and they snuggled together under the bed covers, keeping warm on the drafty winter nights.

I could sense Jerry's emotional pain when he relived this memory and recalled the associated physical aching. Jerry expressed gratitude to his uncle for allowing him to manage the ranch and give him a purpose. He believed he developed a strong work ethic because of this experience, which led him to work hard at every job throughout his long life. To honor his uncle, Jerry named his first and only son after Uncle Press. While Jerry recounted these memories, he seemed to be painfully aware of the abandonment he consequently suffered.

Chester Kylstra, the co-founder of RTF, describes people with an orphan lifestyle as feeling like they lost their home, place of belonging, identity, safety, and peace. They feel lonely, shameful, and fearful of exposure, leading them to control their lives. They have the mistaken belief if they regulate themselves, others, and situations, then others won't find out they are flawed.[4]

While I listened to Chester's MP3 teaching on the orphan lifestyle in 2019, I instantly recalled my parents' words spoken many years earlier. They told me if others knew the real me, they would not want me. I internalized this to mean I must have a hidden, fatal flaw, and I could not risk exposure. Chester was describing me. I lived an orphan lifestyle. I had a Heavenly Father who truly loved and protected me. I also had parents who loved me and provided for me. Still, I felt isolated and somewhat emotionally abandoned at times.

I did not realize until my adult years that my parents felt burdened with emotional woundedness because of painful childhood experiences they thought they had buried. We all were living an orphan lifestyle instead of recognizing our identity is grounded in the Lord. Although I broke off the spirit of abandonment earlier when I learned about inner healing, I understood I also needed the Lord's help to be free from an orphan mindset.

When I was seventeen years old, I contemplated spiritual issues and wondered why God placed us on earth. Was there a reason for the specific time and place of our birth? Surely, we all had a purpose and a destiny to fulfill, so I searched for mine. I was unaware I was seeking my identity. I asked my parents about their purpose, thinking this might help clarify mine. My parents physically stepped back with a look of shock on their faces when I posed my question. You would have thought I physically assaulted them by the reaction their body language suggested. They said they had never heard such an odd question. They both agreed that they were only trying to get through each day and could not think past that.

A few moments after they seemed to somewhat recover from their initial shock at my query, they wanted to know why I asked such a question. Was I unhappy with my life? Should they be worried I was depressed?

I said I did not see life as purposeless and was not sad or discouraged. I was just curious because there appeared to be more to life than I knew or understood. I later realized my parents were probably in survival mode at that time, trying to deal with the pressures each day brought. Little did any of us know then that we were was suffering from the effects of an orphan lifestyle.

The Roots of the Orphan Lifestyle

I learned from RTF that the orphan lifestyle is rooted in rebellion and abandonment. It can begin to operate when a person reaches a point where they feel life is not safe, or their parents cannot protect them or are wounding them. This perception leads to the belief they must care for themselves, so they reject their parents and rebel. When they reject their parents, they perceive their parents abandoned them. Rebellion can also begin in the womb because of a generational curse.[5]

I often have heard the expressions, "To get ahead in this world, you have to take care of number one," and "If you don't take care of number one, who will?" Although the world celebrates independence and self-reliance, this is not God's plan for our lives. God designed us to live in communion with Him. We read in the Bible that Adam and Eve experienced intimate fellowship with God in the Garden of Eden. They had face-to-face encounters with God before the serpent tempted Eve to eat the forbidden fruit. Sonship with God was their identity.

After they disobeyed God and ate the prohibited fruit, they were banished from the Garden and became orphans. Their disobedience and rebellion led to abandonment and rejection, and a cover-up for their shame and fear. They tried to control the situation through blame-shifting. This mistaken orphan identity was passed down the human race. We continue to suffer in our day from the consequences of abandonment, rebellion, disobedience, and rejection, which lead to an orphan lifestyle.[6]

This pattern of self-sufficiency and mistaken identity is evident in our current world. People still grapple with knowing who they belong to and who they are. We no longer need to live as orphans. Jesus told us in John 14:18 that He would not leave us as orphans, and He was sending the Holy Spirit to be with us. God wants to take us from being orphans to our original identity as first-born sons and daughters, but we have to make this choice. Will you accept your birthright and live in it, or will you rebel?

First, acknowledge that you have embraced an orphan mindset. Second, ask the Lord for forgiveness for living your life apart from Him. Third, receive His forgiveness and ask the Holy Spirit to fill you with His presence and guide your next steps. You may need to renounce the lies that you are alone, no one cares about you, or it is up to you to survive.

If you find you cannot forgive yourself and feel bound by shame, fear, and the need to control, ask the Lord's forgiveness for partnering with these spirits. Forgive anyone the Lord brings to your mind that helped influence you to agree with shame, fear, or control. Declare that you are renouncing these negative influences over your life. Finally, invite the Holy Spirit to bless you. Ask Him what He wants to give you in place of the adverse effects.

When you pray this pray aloud, consider reaching your arms out to demonstrate turning your life over to the Lord or laying your life at the foot of Jesus's cross:

> Lord, I repent for believing that I was alone and adopting an orphan mindset. I release myself entirely to You. I forgive my ancestors who believed they were abandoned and developed an orphan heart. I ask the Holy Spirit to nudge me when I attempt to orchestrate my life so I can release myself to You. Only You are in control. I no longer want to be an orphan. Please help me to change my attitude.

Bring to mind any lies I may have believed about myself, so I can renounce them and ask for Your forgiveness. In place of the orphan mindset, I receive adoption into Your family, Lord. I am Your beloved child. Amen.

CHAPTER 19

More Orphan Lifestyle Stories

We prayed with numerous people who had rebelled when they were physically abandoned by one or both parents and believed they needed to fend for themselves. This pattern was evident in many of the men who experienced incarceration. Often, their fathers abandoned the family, or one or both parents relocated for a better life, with the promise the family would join them when feasible. Reuniting with the family did not always work out, and when it did, there typically were years of separation first.

Marcus expressed profound grief over never having contact with his father, who left the family before his birth. He told us about the years he waited at the docks as a young boy hoping to catch a glimpse of his father after he came off a container ship. He saw his father's photo and knew he worked on container ships but never met him. His mother sent him to live with an aunt at age five when she moved to the United States to earn money, hoping for a better life for her family.

He described his young life as chaotic and lonely when he searched for his place in the world. He felt unprotected and vulnerable, which led to victimization and issues controlling his anger. Later in early adulthood, Marcus was diagnosed with Post Traumatic Stress Disorder and attended classes on anger management.

When asked what he wanted Jesus to do for him during prayer, Marcus initially said he desired to be reunited with his family and to have more understanding of God's Word. While he bowed his head in prayer, his 6-foot 6-inch frame shook uncontrollably, and tears streamed down his face for several moments. Marcus instantly pictured himself back at the docks as a young boy. Only this time, he met his father. For several minutes, Marcus was speechless. He was astonished that the Lord gave him a vision of meeting the man he searched for all his life.

Struggling to describe the physical sensation that overwhelmed him, Marcus said it felt like someone pulled something off his body. He had not experienced anything like this before when praying. His face beamed when he told us of his gratefulness to the Lord for this prayer time. Marcus believed the Lord released the pain of abandonment and showed him that He had been with him waiting at the docks, protecting him. Marcus was no longer an orphan but rather a son of the Lord of the universe.

Otis experienced feelings of abandonment, shame, fear, rejection, bitterness, and guilt. He felt as though he navigated life without a rudder and needed direction. During healing prayer, Otis asked the Lord to change his life and show him the next steps.

He recalled his mother enduring beatings from his dad until he abandoned the family when Otis was six. Overwhelmed and angry at her husband for the abuse and desertion, she lashed out at Otis, who was the spitting image of his dad. In a fit of rage, she beat Otis and screamed she should have aborted him. He learned that his dad had given his mother pills to abort him. Later, he lived with an aunt and endured more physical beatings until his mother remarried when Otis was thirteen.

Otis loved his stepdad and sensed a feeling of belonging and acceptance in the family for the first time at age thirteen. Unfortunately, this sense of security did not last long. His stepdad was killed by gang members while driving a bus when Otis was fifteen. Otis said he was supposed to be on that bus too, but he did not ride that day for some reason unknown to him at the time.

While Otis continued to share his life story with us, it became apparent the Lord had intervened multiple times to protect him. Several years later, the police thwarted his plan to avenge the gang member who killed his stepdad. He chose probation and school completion and became the first person in his family to earn a university degree. Gang members continued to threaten his life, so he escaped to the United States, leaving his wife and child behind until he could arrange for them to join him. Otis said he felt guilty because he did not keep the promises he made to God.

Otis said he was now aware that generational patterns of abandonment, abuse, anger, and condemnation were evident in his current family. He wanted this to stop so his children and wife would not continue to experience this pain. He declared, "No more orphan lifestyle."

After Otis broke the negative ancestral influences, he asked the Lord's forgiveness for any part he played in allowing these patterns in his life. He also broke unhealthy soul ties. Otis expressed gratitude to the Lord for saving his life several times and asked Him to remove the guilt he felt.

Several men described suffering emotional abandonment as children, which led to rejection and feelings of unworthiness.

Cecil never felt like he belonged in the family after his dad told him he most likely was not his son. His dad tried to convince him he was switched at birth at the hospital and belonged to another family. This pronouncement left Cecil bewildered, wondering if this was true or just another slam from his dad, who had already abandoned the family. Cecil's dad left home when Cecil was three years old after multiple instances of physical abuse directed at his mother. Broken relationships, rejection, addiction, and the consequences of bad choices plagued Cecil throughout the following years.

Cecil desperately wanted to receive peace and relief from constant distressing emotions. He accepted Jesus as his Savior when we prayed and asked God to help him forgive his parents. His body shook when I placed my hands on his shoulders and asked the Lord to give him peace. He said he pictured himself on a football field filled with light and knew that light was God. He asked us to guide him in prayers of forgiveness to break unhealthy soul ties, and negative patterns in his family associated with rejection, abandonment, addiction, sexual sin, and the occult. The Lord healed his broken heart, and Cecil experienced the peace he sought.

When we met Sebastian through the prison ministry, we asked, "What would you like Jesus to do for you today?" He tearfully responded, "I do not feel like I am worth anything. I need Jesus to transform my life."

At that point, Sebastian told us his life story, highlighting the events he thought led him to feel insignificant. He explained he was the eleventh and youngest child in his family. His dad never signed papers acknowledging him as his son, which left Sebastian feeling illegitimate. Although his dad did not physically leave the family, he beat his wife, frequently yelled at the children, and did not provide for their financial needs. Sebastian praised his mother for instilling good values and for her self-sacrificing nature.

Sebastian left home to live with his girlfriend at a young age, believing he finally found a place where he belonged and was valued. They had a daughter, but the romantic bond soon became strained. He described numerous incidents where his girlfriend lied about their daughter's health attempting to manipulate him into staying in the relationship.

While in that relationship, Sebastian met someone else, and a similar pattern of manipulation and lying ensued. He sought comfort from alcohol, which only exacerbated his problems and led to addiction. Rocky relationships continued when he fathered two more children with two other women. Sebastian worried he was treating his girlfriends and children in the same hurtful manner that his father treated him.

We explained the concepts of generational curses and ungodly soul ties and the importance of forgiveness. Sebastian recognized that the spirit of abandonment operated in his family line. The feelings of neglect, shame, and unworthiness that he despised now impacted his children. Sebastian did not want them to go through the heartache he experienced most of his life. We led Sebastian in the prayer to break ancestral curses associated with abandonment, unworthiness, addiction, sexual sin, trauma, and abuse.

He also cut the unhealthy connections with his father and the women he had been intimate with outside of marriage. Sebastian prayed blessings on each person he forgave and received God's blessings in place of the generational curses he renounced. He now understood that he was adopted into God's family and had a place of belonging as a beloved son.

Antonio described himself as a "solitary person" and was determined at age twenty-four not to let any more heartache permeate his life. He grew up with his mother and five older brothers who had three different fathers. Antonio never knew his birth father. His older brothers and mother worked to support the family, often leaving him home alone.

Being alone provided an opportunity for victimization by a relative. The resulting shame led to drug and alcohol addiction in an attempt to mask the humiliation. One time when Antonio was eight, a priest came to his home to visit because they were not attending church. Although this appeared to be a caring gesture, Anthony stopped attending church after the priest humiliated him in front of others. Traumatic events continued to afflict the family, and gang members reportedly killed two of his brothers' fathers.

Antonio recognized something was missing from his insulated life. Self-sufficiency was no longer working. He was imprisoned in his thoughts and physically housed in a jail cell. He could not provide for his one-year-old son and girlfriend while incarcerated and worried about their welfare. Antonio said he was ready to ask the Lord for help. He emphatically declared he did not want his son to feel the pain of desertion he endured.

After breaking generational curses associated with abandonment, shame, abuse, trauma, and the occult, Antonio felt the Lord's peace. He described feeling a tremendous weight lift off him after forgiving his father for leaving him and his mother. Antonio also forgave the people who shamed him—the priest who ridiculed him and the relative who abused him.

Gus said he accepted Jesus as his Savior seven years before we met him. As a result of never feeling connected to his family, he learned to control his life. His grandparents mistreated him and repeatedly told him that his mother became pregnant with him by another man before marrying their son. They exclaimed it was evident that he looked nothing like them. In his teen years, his cousins taunted him by saying he did not look like them, and they wanted nothing to do with him. Despised and rejected, Gus turned to alcohol and women for comfort.

He recognized he was repeating the same unhealthy patterns raising his children that he endured as a child. Gus wanted the pain of abandonment and rejection to stop now so his children would not continue to experience this agony. He recommitted his life to the Lord while we prayed. We led him in prayers to break the negative generational influences associated with abandonment, anger, rejection, addiction, sexual sin, and the occult. Gus asked the Lord to direct his life and to help him establish new healthy patterns. He requested the Lord to come into his life and be the father he never had. The Lord graciously answered his prayer. No more orphan lifestyle.

After seeing the Lord physically heal several people in a prison church service, Benito requested healing prayer. We asked him what he wanted Jesus to do for him when we met for his prayer appointment. Immediately, tears began to flow, and he said, "so much to do." He witnessed numerous instances of physical abuse, loss, and illness over the past thirty-six years.

Benito had been hospitalized as a child and required surgery to insert a tube so he could eat. His sister died because of a brain tumor when he was fifteen, and now his mother was seriously ill. Benito feared his mother might die. He told us his biological father wanted a girl and left when he was born, so he never knew his father. His mother had been adopted and did not know her birth parents. A spirit of abandonment appeared to be operating in this family.

He also told us he wanted to know the Jesus he heard about who heals so that he could commit his life to Him. With closed eyes and a bowed head, Benito asked Jesus to come into his heart. He told us that he felt Jesus's presence next to him and sensed the Lord holding his hand. Benito expressed astonishment at sensing light when his eyes were closed. He exclaimed all he saw in the past was darkness when he tried to close his eyes to pray.

Benito told us about the destruction caused by generational influences of abandonment, rejection, abuse, sexual sin, infirmity, and death in his family line. He adamantly declared he did not want these patterns to continue when he married and had a family. Benito asked us to lead him in prayer to break the power of these influences over his life and his future family. He left the prayer session feeling forgiven and blessed by the Lord.

Brendan first learned about his birth father at age twelve after his teachers called home to tell his parents he was not doing well in school. He was easily distracted and unable to complete his schoolwork, which led to failing grades. Exasperated and out of strategies to help Brendan, his teachers asked his parents if anyone else in the family demonstrated learning challenges and distractibility. His parents said they did not have information about Brendan's birth father because a stranger assaulted his mother and got her pregnant.

The next day at school, Brendan's teachers told him they learned a gang member had raped his mother. They suggested perhaps this was the reason he was a poor student. He was shocked to learn the man he called father for twelve years was not his birth father. Brendan believed he was an accident and should never have been born. He accepted the pronouncement that he was a weak student and would always be unsuccessful because he had a poor attention span.

When Brendan shared these feelings and thoughts with the Lord in prayer, he realized these were lies. After all, he had successfully completed a college program in graphic design. He broke the lie that he is distractible and asked for forgiveness for allowing this lie to influence him. More importantly, Brendan now saw himself as a valued son of the Lord and not as an accident. Brendan accepted Jesus as his Lord and Savior during prayer and broke generational curses associated with violence, abuse, and sexual sin.

Not all of the men at the prison who described feeling a sense of abandonment and rejection had fathers who left the family. Several had mothers who left or even both parents who left for various reasons.

Al's mother left home when he was three months old, and his father subsequently left when he was three years old. Sent to live with his paternal grandmother, Al learned to fend for himself. He endured abuse from another adult relative at age nine, which left him traumatized and depressed. Al suffered from feelings of worthlessness and self-loathing. He had virtually no contact with his mother until she encouraged him to join a gang at age fourteen. She and her siblings were active in local gangs that provided a sense of belonging. They tried to persuade Al to join, promising a sense of camaraderie and protection.

Fearing for his safety at age fifteen, Al's grandmother sent him to the United States, where he reconnected with his father. Al's father had married a loving woman who treated Al like a son. Despite this new sense of belonging, he still felt restless and unsure of himself and his place in the world.

During our prayer time, Al rededicated his life to the Lord and asked Jesus to help him feel better. He broke several negative ancestral influences, including abandonment, violence, addiction, depression, trauma, rejection, and self-condemnation. He also broke unhealthy soul ties with the relative who abused him. Although this relative died several years earlier, he needed to break the unhealthy spiritual connection between them to experience freedom.

Eugene never knew his birth mother. His grandmother told him that she had died, but he did not know anything about the circumstances of her death. All Eugene had of his mother was one photograph. He later learned she had another child, but he did not know his half-sibling. Eugene's father moved to the United States when he was a young child leaving him in his grandmother's care. She raised him and took Eugene to church with her every night.

Eugene came to the United States in his twenties searching for his dad. They had a few phone conversations, and he saw a few photos of his dad before their first meeting. Eugene had such high hopes for this reunion, expecting his dad to be delighted when they finally saw each other in person. He envisioned receiving profuse apologies for the lost years, followed by his father begging his forgiveness and asking to start over again and be the dad he always wanted.

This imagined scenario did not happen, and Eugene said he felt his dad was a stranger who had no love for him. In an attempt to bond, his dad offered to take him shopping that day, but Eugene refused the invitation.

After this disappointing encounter, Eugene contacted his dad, asking to meet one more time. He knew his dad was in the vicinity visiting his daughter, a half-sister Eugene never met. Eugene hoped his dad would come to his home to meet his infant son. As soon as Eugene laid eyes on his dad, tears streamed down his face. All he felt was sadness that his dad had not initiated the visit. Eugene was so proud of his infant son, so why was his father not overjoyed to see him? Why had he not searched for Eugene? His dad told him that he did not have the time or the money to help him, and he did not understand why Eugene cried so much. His dad declared that he did not get much from his father (meaning Eugene's grandfather), yet he did not weep.

Eugene interpreted his father's reaction to mean he was disappointed because he was not the son he expected. He wanted to forgive his father and start the relationship over, but he did not know how to do this. Eugene was afraid that his anger and disappointment would come through again and spoil any future visits.

During prayer, he asked Jesus to help him talk to his dad to find out what happened and how they could move forward. Eugene broke generational curses associated with spirits of abandonment, addiction, rejection, and shame and asked the Lord to change his orphan mindset.

Eugene expressed gratitude for the church assisting his wife and child with expenses while he remained imprisoned. His wife promised to stay with him even if the court rendered a deportation decision. He thanked the Lord for his wife. More importantly, Eugene thanked the Lord for the assurance that He would never leave or forsake him.

We prayed for each person to continue to lean on the Lord for His guidance—through the good times and bad times. We knew the enemy would try to steal the peace and joy they just experienced and cause them to doubt their identity as sons and daughters of the Lord. We also prayed for spiritually healthy Christian mentors to walk beside them as they began their journey as new creations in the Lord. Old habits of self-sufficiency and orchestrating their lives would likely resurface, and they needed to be prepared to fight against these.

I knew from personal experience that it is easy to slip into taking back areas of our lives that we relinquished to the Lord. There were numerous times when I cried out to the Lord that I wanted Him to be the Lord of my life and permitted Him to take complete control. But when a challenging situation arose, typically concerning a family member, I attempted to solve the problem independently. What happened to my relinquishing the reins and leaning on the Lord for everything?

Our prayer partner, Marty, suggested a prophetic act to demonstrate our giving control of a troubling circumstance to the Lord. We were worried about our adult children. We had both prayed and heard the Lord tell us that He had our children's backs, and we could trust Him to take care of them. They were no longer our responsibility. We needed to take our hands off the current situations and give our children to Jesus.

Marty asked us to take framed photos of our children and place them on the table, symbolizing our act of obedience giving them to Jesus. We were not abandoning our children but rather showing that they belonged to Jesus, and we trusted Him with their lives. In a sense, this was similar to placing our troubles on the Lord's altar or at Jesus's feet.

A sense of peace filled our hearts and minds when we turned our children over to Jesus. I wish I could tell you that I continually maintained this posture, but I haven't. It requires a daily resetting of our thoughts on the Lord. Believing we are in control of anything is an illusion. Yes, the Lord does give us free will, and we can choose to ignore Him. Deciding to discount God will not bode well for us. The Lord is ready and waiting for us to come back to Him. We can count on His promises. He will not abandon us. He is the solution to all of our difficulties. Do you need to turn your life over to the Lord?

Pray this prayer aloud:

> As I read the stories of others with an orphan lifestyle, I was reminded that some negative ancestral spirits have operated in my lineage. I repent on behalf of my ancestors, who allowed these negative influences into our family line. Lord, I ask You to forgive me for any part I played in embracing the orphan mindset. I receive Your forgiveness, Lord. Help me to reset my thoughts on You daily. Thank you for calling me Your beloved child. I know that I have a place of belonging in You, and You will never leave or abandon me. You are my source of identity, safety, and peace. Amen.

Nothing Can Separate You from God's Love

God cannot love you any less than He already does, no matter what you have done or think about yourself. He is madly in love with you, and He desires to be in a relationship with you. There is nothing that can separate you from His love. He is your place of belonging, identity, safety, and peace. Even if your parents could not love you the way you needed, the Lord loves and cherishes you.

CHAPTER 20

It's Not Too Late

A well-known prophet came to our church in the summer of 2018 to speak about prophecy and hearing from the Lord. At the close of one of his teaching sessions, he announced he did not have time to give each attendee a personal word from the Lord, but he wanted to pray a blessing over each individual. We formed a horizontal line in front of the altar, ready to accept whatever God had for us. Most people bowed their heads and held their hands out in a posture ready to receive from the Lord. The prophet briefly stood in front of each person, putting his hand on their forehead while he prayed.

After blessing me, he walked to the person on my left and silently prayed over her. Then he turned to look back at me, and with a grin on his face, said, "It's not too late." When I looked up at him for clarification, he chuckled and said he didn't know what it meant, but the Lord specifically highlighted that phrase for me. He indicated he acted in obedience to the Lord's direction to share this despite his comment about not having time to give personal words. He then continued to walk down the line and silently pray over the remaining people.

Those four words spoke encouragement to my heart. There were relationships I desperately hoped to see restored for years but was discouraged because this had not happened, and I lost hope. Perhaps it was not too late to rebuild these connections. Often, we do not see change occurring with our natural eyes when a transformation is occurring spiritually. I was optimistic that this might be the case.

I had silently questioned whether God could still use me, a sixty-five-year-old recently retired university professor. I wanted to serve the Lord and use whatever time He granted me to help further His kingdom through healing prayer. The last five months of teaching while receiving chemotherapy for lymphoma were rough and convinced me that I had made the correct decision to retire. In August 2018, I still had sixteen more months of immunotherapy left to complete the prescribed treatment protocol. Fortunately, this treatment did not have the adverse side effects the chemotherapy had. Physically, I was doing well.

I was acutely aware that I must have placed much of my self-worth and purpose in my teaching, a position I no longer held. I was somewhat uncertain what the future held for me since I no longer had that identity in this unsettled transition period. I had many conversations with the Lord over the previous few months about what was next for me.

Many questions surfaced. Did I really hear clearly from the Lord that it was time to retire? Did God still have more for me to do? Had I missed something?

I began to understand that I again looked to others to define me. My true identity was not a university professor, researcher, department chairperson, psychologist, or any of the titles or academic certifications I achieved. Those accomplishments were not the focus of what lay ahead for me. The Lord was pursuing me to rest in Him and enjoy our time together—being in a relationship with Him. But what would that look like? I did not know. I was accustomed *to doing* and not *being*. I had not rested long enough before this time to understand how this might unfold.

You may recall that I lived with an orphan mindset for far too many years, trying to orchestrate my life. Now was the perfect time to practice what I had learned about my real identity in Christ and trust Him to show me the next steps. I did not need to know the whole plan in advance as I once thought.

The Lord would not let me down, and He always had a better plan. None of my mistakes or previous attempts to choreograph my life separated me from the Lord who pursued me. It was not too late for me to start over.

More confirmation came during that conference weekend when another guest speaker asked those in the audience who needed physical healing to come forward so he could pray for them. My husband, and friend, Maria, encouraged me to step out of the pew to receive prayer.

The speaker prayed for health and the elimination of disease for each person who came to him. When I stood in front of him, he did not say anything about my physical health. Instead, he surprised me by saying, "You are being re-fired. There is an anointing over you. You are a teacher, and you will be preaching. I do not know you, and we have not met before. But the Lord highlighted you to me several times today. Others have maligned you, but the Lord is restoring."

Although we had not previously met, that speaker addressed my two pressing concerns. The Lord used both men during this conference to let me know that He had not forgotten me. There was still a destiny and call on my life. I was not too old to be used for service in God's kingdom. Furthermore, the Lord promised to restore my broken heart and fractured relationships due to false accusations.

He can do the same for you—no matter what you did in your past, regardless of what others said about you or how old or young you are. If you have any questions regarding your identity, I suggest you read and listen to The Father's Love Letter, found online at https://www.fathersloveletter.com/ for encouragement and God's truth about you. It is a compilation of paraphrased Bible verses from the Old and New Testaments written and audibly recorded in the form of a love letter from Father God to you. He says you are His precious child, and He is longing to have a relationship with you.

Paul tells us in Romans 8:38–39, "For I am sure that neither death nor life, nor angels nor rulers, nor things present nor things to come, nor powers, nor height nor depth, nor anything else in all creation, will be able to separate us from the love of God in Christ Jesus our Lord."

But What About My Limitations?

Do not despair because you have some imperfections. We all carry some wounding and inadequacies. God still has a purpose for your life. He can use your personality and your life experiences along with the abilities, talents, and gifts He gave you for His glory. You do not need to wait to approach Him until you feel good enough.

Remember, the Lord qualifies those He calls. Randy Clark declares God uses our weaknesses to demonstrate His delight in using broken vessels. By God's grace alone, we are qualified.[1] You and I are in good company when we consider the people God chose in the Bible. God turned Moses, who murdered a man, into a leader who brought the Israelites out of Egypt. Even though Moses stuttered, God used him to speak to His people mightily.

Several women in Kansas City asked me to lead a Christian women's group in the late 1990s. My initial reaction was panic because I was sure I was not a good public speaker. I told them I could not possibly fulfill this role that required me to address and lead a large group of women. They asked me to pray about this because they believed the Lord put my name on their hearts.

When I prayed about their request, I felt the Lord did want me to accept this position despite my fear. Of course, I initially reminded the Lord I never formally took a public speaking course or even a speech class in college, even though I earned several college degrees. Secretly, I was hoping this might disqualify me.

The same women who asked me to lead their group also playfully teased me about my New York accent. Didn't the Lord realize I needed to do a lot of public speaking if I accepted this position? Wouldn't my accent be an issue? Of course, I laugh about this now and feel convinced God must have a sense of humor when He listens to us telling Him what He already knows. After all, He knows everything about us. And yet, we often believe we need to give Him reminders. Then I sensed the Lord bring Moses to my mind.

Moses used a similar argument regarding his challenges with speaking eloquently when the Lord chose him. I certainly did not believe I was even remotely on a level close to Moses, the prophet. That prompting from the Lord certainly got my attention. All I could say at the time was God must undoubtedly have a lot of patience in addition to a sense of humor.

If you are frustrated thinking it is too late for a restart or fearful that God cannot use you—think again. I did accept the position to lead the Christian women's group, and the Lord helped me. Did I always speak eloquently? No. Did I always know what to do? No. But the Lord sent other women who had more experience to assist me. We may be practicing new skills, such as public speaking or leading a group, but the Holy Spirit is never practicing. He will make sure our audience hears what He wants them to understand, no matter how articulate our speech is. Remember, the challenging times we spend here on earth developing our character are short compared to when we will be with the Lord in eternity.

Pray this prayer aloud:

> Thank you, Lord, for relentlessly pursuing me and never leaving me. Please forgive me for focusing on my limitations and believing they disqualified me from Your service. You gave several examples in the Bible of people who were flawed that You called and qualified. I trust You will equip me for work in Your kingdom when we partner together. I am grateful to be considered Your beloved child based on my identity in You, Lord, and not on my merit. Amen.

CHAPTER 21

You Can Depend on God

Perhaps you are questioning whether you can trust God. Will He be there when you need Him? If other key people in our lives have let us down or were angry toward us, we may attribute these same characteristics to God. Christian author, Philip Yancey, writes when we face crises in our lives, and God seems to be silent, we become disappointed. No one is exempt from the downward spiral of disappointment. A seed of doubt is then planted, followed by a response of anger or betrayal. We question whether we can depend on God. Yancey contends that we silently ask if God is unfair, silent, and hidden.[2]

If you have been there in despair and discontent with God, you are not alone. The Bible is full of stories depicting people searching for answers from God amid calamity. God clearly understands our distress. He sent Jesus to earth to live as a man and experience emotions just as we do. Jesus also endured tremendous unfairness during His time here. So, yes, the Lord understands our pain. He's been there too. God provided a way for us when we experience disasters and injustice—through reliance on Jesus.

Remember the story of Job in the Bible? He endured horrific tragedy, losing his children, servants, and animals. Then he was inflicted with painful skin diseases. God was not punishing Job—yet, He allowed Job to endure these miseries. God did not prevent the hardships, but in the end, He restored Job's friendships, doubled his fortune, gave him ten more children and 140 more years. Job's story reminds us that God will heal all illnesses at the end of time, evil will be punished or forgiven, and fairness will reign.

In the meantime, we need to trust God and His promises, even if we cannot see them. Job did. Our troubles on earth are temporary compared to the time we spend in eternity when God will right all the wrongs. Yancey reminds the reader that we sometimes perceive God as unfair because we live in a world bound by time. God transcends time and sees the whole picture—we do not. Yancy believes when the earth passes and the course of history is over, we will understand how God worked all things together for good. Until then, we need to have faith even if we do not have direct evidence of God working in our lives.[3]

We heard countless stories of how God intervened in the lives of people we were blessed to encounter in the healing prayer ministry. Miracles are still happening. Sometimes God's intervention was immediately recognized, and other times it was not acknowledged until later when the person took time to reflect on their life. Others were waiting for God to move in their lives as they had seen Him do for others.

God is Still Active in Our Lives

Many of the men we met through the prison ministry recounted times in their lives when they believed God had saved them from a tragic outcome. Although all the men thanked God for intervening in their lives, their willingness to surrender their lives to Him varied.

Julio's prayer request was for Jesus to change his life. He grew up in Central America, the youngest of four children. When he was thirty months old, his family sought safety in the shelter of another home in a nearby town while a hurricane raged in their locality. When the storm was over, they left the shelter to return home. They needed to walk across an old, wooden overpass to get back home. Unfortunately, the rickety bridge collapsed when Julio and his family were on it, plunging Julio and his brother into the deep river. A stranger jumped into the rapidly moving water and rescued Julio and his brother.

Julio recounted several other times when he thought God saved him from severe injury and imminent death. Although he understood that the Lord interceded for him, something still held him back from fully embracing all the Lord had for him. During prayer, Julio asked the Lord to help him change his behavior. He thanked God for saving his life multiple times. He said he was not yet ready to turn his life completely over to the Lord. We blessed him and prayed for others to come into his life who could water the seeds already planted regarding the saving power of Jesus.

Leonardo desperately wanted to remain in the United States. He feared he would be killed if he returned to his birthplace. His lawyer tried to reverse his deportation order but was unsuccessful. When Leonardo arrived at the airport with several other men to board the plane for their deportation to Central America, he was the only one not permitted to enter the aircraft. No one explained why he was not deported that evening and sent back to jail. Now convinced that God saved his life and gave him another chance to start over, Leonardo decided to accept Jesus as his Lord and Savior during our prayer time.

Santiago believed that God was still active in people's lives because he witnessed miracles. Several years earlier, he traveled to church on a bus that plunged over an embankment causing forty-six of the sixty passengers to lose their lives. Santiago survived, but four of his cousins perished. Convalescing from extensive injuries gave him time to reflect on his life, and he whole-heartedly believed that God saved him for a purpose and blessed him with an improved relationship with his father.

Unfortunately, shortly after Santiago's release from the hospital, his father died, leaving him to grieve deeply over the loss of the connection they developed. He turned to alcohol and associated with others who took advantage of him, leading to his eventual arrest. During prayer, Santiago broke ancestral influences related to poverty, victimization, addiction, trauma, death, abandonment, and ungodly sexual activity. He asked Jesus for wisdom to direct his life on a new path and for the Holy Spirit to fill him. He left the prayer session with a new lease on life.

We continued to see evidence of God's goodness when we prayed with people, and they shared their stories. Francisco said he never bonded with his dad, who suffered from alcoholism and left the family. His mother raised the children alone and could not financially provide for their basic needs. She left without warning for the United States when Francisco was five years old, promising to return for him in one month. He did not understand why she deserted him and once again felt forsaken. Five years later, she sent money to bring him and his sister to the United States.

Francisco described his life as unsettled. He turned to drugs and alcohol to ease his emotional pain and now wanted freedom from addiction. He did not want his future family to experience the depression and sense of abandonment he suffered. Francisco prayed for Jesus to give him peace and free him from his alcohol dependence. His told us his dad contacted him on his deathbed and asked for forgiveness for abandoning the family. If his earthly father could do this, he knew his Heavenly Father would do more for him.

Roberto told us about his losses—his father's death, his mother's illness, his brother's incarceration, and the loss of his home. Roberto said he and his brother wanted to take revenge on the person who took their home and belongings, leaving their family to suffer. His father stopped them from enacting retaliation on two occasions. Miraculously, people arrived to build a new house, double the original home's size and value. Roberto strongly believed Jesus sent the people to bless his family and restore their dwelling.

He also prayed and fasted later when the judge sentenced him to prison for eighteen months. Amazingly, the authorities lessened his sentence, and Roberto credited God for reducing his prison term. During our prayer time, he forgave the people who falsely accused him of stealing, which resulted in his imprisonment. Roberto declared he now wanted to tell others about the goodness of God, who brings restoration even when we do not deserve His blessings.

We could sense Cristóbal's exuberance when we met him for prayer. He told us he had permission to remain in the United States and was scheduled to leave the prison that afternoon. He could not wait to be with his family again and play with his four-year-old daughter. After receiving three deportation orders, Cristobal's lawyer informed him there was no chance he could stay in the United States unless God interceded with a miracle. God did intervene, and Cristobal would soon be a free man.

Lateef's encounter with an angel of the Lord was one of the most unforgettable stories we heard. Lateef was a successful business owner with a wife and three daughters when he gave his life to Jesus. His Muslim family disowned him. Because of his new faith, he was driven out of his country, forced to leave his home, extended family, and prosperous business behind. The night before Lateef went to the embassy in his country to obtain a visa to the United States, he had a dream.

The following day, he arrived at the embassy stunned to see the man from his dream sitting behind a desk. The man, David, helped him complete the necessary forms and assured Lateef that he would soon receive his visa to leave the country.

When Lateef joyfully contacted the embassy the next day to thank David, they said they never had a person with that name or description working there. Lateef believed David was an angel sent by God to protect him and his family.

Lateef started another business in the United States and was able to provide well for his family. Prosperity did not last long, and he and his family faced many hardships. His daughter was diagnosed with cancer. Lateef's new business partner was caught in illegal activity and falsely blamed Lateef, which resulted in his incarceration. Although Lateef won his court case, technicalities delayed his release for many months. In the meantime, his wife left their home and returned to Islam, and Lateef suffered two heart attacks in jail.

When we met Lateef again, he told us that his release was finally scheduled for the following week, and his daughter was doing well after several surgeries. He asked us to pray with him for his wife to rededicate her life to Christ. He forgave the people who falsely accused him and rejected him. Although we did not see Lateef again, the chaplains assured us that he was safely released to his family when we returned the following week.

Good Can Come from Difficult Circumstances

Several men in the prison facility told us they believed that incarceration saved their lives. Their lives were moving swiftly out of control before their arrests. Rather than viewing imprisonment as punishment, they saw it as an opportunity to reflect on their lives, lean on the Lord, and start over. They knew in their hearts that God had not abandoned them and waited for their return to Him.

Kendall witnessed his grandfather's murder and his sister's attempted murder before coming to the United six years earlier in the hope of finding a better life. He struggled with intense fears, anger, and frequent nightmares since that traumatic incident. The police arrested him when they saw his erratic driving and suspected Kendall was intoxicated. He was unsure what came over him that day, but he knew something was radically wrong, and he could not make any rational decisions.

We asked Jesus to remove the trauma and fear off Kendall's body from that horrific evening years ago. Kendall also broke generational curses associated with addiction, abandonment, ungodly sexual activity, fear, violence, and murder. He forgave the gunmen and broke several unhealthy soul ties. Kendall felt the Lord's peace and the trauma lift off his body during prayer. He believed God saved his life when arrested, and he expressed his gratitude to the Lord for a new beginning.

Donnie came to the United States alone twelve years earlier to escape violence and gang activity. He admitted to making some bad choices and expressed thankfulness to the Lord for His forgiveness. Police had arrested him after an altercation with his wife. Shortly after his arrest, his wife changed her mind and wanted the charges against Donnie dropped. Police said this was not possible.

He told us he was thankful for the incarceration because his life on the outside was in danger. He was a changed man and was now teaching a Bible study to his fellow inmates. He wanted them to know that God was good and had protected him. Imprisonment was not God's punishment. His jail sentence saved his life and gave him time to focus on the Lord and share his testimony. He wanted the other men to know that God would protect and forgive them if they turned to Him.

Kendall and Donnie could have remained bitter over their arrests and the unfair events they suffered, but they chose to reframe their situations and focus on God's goodness. If you suffer from injustice, bring your fears and concerns to the Lord. He has all the answers, and He is still performing miracles today.

Pray this prayer aloud:

> Lord, thank you that You are still the God of miracles and are active in my life. You will never leave me or forsake me. I can count on Your promises. Please help me put my trust in You daily and remember good can come from the difficult circumstances I face. I am more than a conqueror in You. Amen.

CHAPTER 22

God is Bigger Than Our Problems

P ress has often said our current life is the training ground for our lives in eternity. We are not promised a comfortable life while on earth, so we should not be surprised when facing challenges.

Rick Warren suggests the Lord's ultimate goal for our lives on earth is character development. We are to grow spiritually, more like Christ. When we forget this, we become frustrated with our circumstances and focus on our problems.[4] Warren emphasizes everything that happens to us has spiritual significance. The Scriptures tell us all our days were written in God's book before we were born. (See Psalm 139:16.)[5] Instead of referring to circumstances that some people would consider coincidences, Press and I like to call them God instances.

We can take comfort in knowing nothing that happens to us is a surprise to the Lord. Perhaps some of the difficult situations we face are tests we need to master to move on to the next character development phase. All we will take to Heaven is our character—indeed, not our possessions. Why not reframe our problems as opportunities to enhance our personality? Ask the Lord what He is trying to teach or show you when you face trials and tribulations. Lean into the Lord first instead of succumbing to worry and anxiety. Romans 8:28 reminds us that God causes everything to work together for good for those who love God and are called to His purpose, which is to become more like Jesus.

The Bible tells us Jesus endured many challenges and was tempted, rejected, and criticized. We also face experiences similar to those Jesus confronted. Hebrews 5:8–9 tells us Jesus learned obedience through suffering. Problems also compel us to look to God and depend on Him instead of ourselves. We can be encouraged by the realization none of our problems occurred without God's permission. Even if the difficulties we endure are meant for evil by the enemy, God can use those situations for good. We can take comfort because we do not navigate life by ourselves or without a rudder or a compass. God is aware of everything. He is omniscient, omnipotent, and omnipresent. Scripture tells us He even knows the number of hairs on our heads. (See Luke 12:7.)

Often, the people we prayed with dealt with severe hardships and felt their only hope was a miracle. Several men from war-torn countries overseas endured physical torture and near-fatal attempts on their lives. To stay alive, they needed to flee their countries, often leaving families behind while they narrowly escaped with only the clothes on their backs. Their difficulties continued when they tried to navigate a safe passage through several countries in search of asylum. Their journeys often lasted several months and were fraught with danger traveling through jungles and deserts, only to be met by bandits who robbed them and left them alone and injured. Despite the significant challenges, they knew the Lord protected them and would never leave them. They held on to God's promise to supply their every need in Jesus Christ. (See Philippians 4:19.)

Nelson said that he appreciated every government that allowed him to pass through their country. After traveling for over four months, authorities denied him initial entrance into the United States, leading him to fear deportation. He later learned the delay was because he needed medical treatment for high blood pressure.

His prayer requests when we met were for safety, closeness to Jesus, and the power to do the Lord's will. I sensed the Lord wanted him to know that he was a man of valor, tenacity, and courage. When Nelson made his prayer requests known to the Lord, he sensed that he would be serving in God's kingdom with Jesus protecting children.

Although Ronald was from the same country as Nelson, they did not meet until both were in the U.S. seeking asylum. Ronald accepted Jesus as his Lord and Savior thirteen years earlier. He recently married, completed his college degree, and had a successful business. Shortly after this time of prosperity, the military broke into his home and beat and shot him. He fled to the bush for safety for several weeks and then embarked on an arduous journey searching for refuge. Ronald had been away from his home for nine months when we met him. His wife had a baby in his absence, and he had no idea how she and their newborn baby were doing.

Ronald worried about his family, who remained in their home country amidst the chaos and violence. He heard that the military set his home ablaze, and his wife and children fled to his mother-in-law's house for safety.

He asked the Lord to bless him and grant him asylum and good health. He desired to live a Christ-like life and raise his children to be like Jesus. He told us he was close to completing a correspondence Bible course and proudly showed us his high exam scores. Despite the terrible circumstances in his life, Ronald still wanted to serve the Lord. He believed in the Lord's promise in Jeremiah 29:11, which says, "For I know the plans I have for you, declares the Lord, plans for welfare and not for evil, to give you a future and a hope."

Other men told us about times in their lives when they knew the Lord helped them, but they then turned away from Him.

Carlos accepted Jesus as his Savior the year before we met him. Although his thoughts changed in a positive direction, he said his behavior did not change significantly, and he struggled with old habits. Recurrent nightmares of being attacked plagued him for the past five years.

He asked for a prayer appointment because he wanted Jesus to change his lifestyle—no more drugs. When he asked the Lord for healing, Jesus took him to a memory when he was fifteen years old, and someone shot him while on the soccer field. Carlos thought death was imminent, and he would never see his parents again. Then Jesus showed him how He intervened and saved his life that night. Carlos finally believed that God was not holding his past misbehavior against him and had restored him.

When we met William, he immediately told us he struggled with tremendous anxiety because he was scheduled for deportation back to Central America. He feared for his life if he returned. William said his home country could not find his records when it came time for his deportation the previous week.

With our translator's help, William told us we had prayed with him several weeks earlier, and he did not sign up for this second prayer session. At that point, we recalled praying earlier with a man with the same first name who had an angry countenance and who had described experiences with excessive violence.

At the end of that first prayer session, William's facial expression changed, and he appeared less agitated and calmer after forgiving his abusers. We did not initially recognize him this second time, but here he was again for prayer. William did not look as angry as when we first met him. Perhaps this was a divine appointment.

William said he called his mother to relay his fear and anxiety over his current deportation situation. His mother told him that her church friend said he needed to reconcile with the Lord. William smiled and said he believed this second prayer session must have been meant to be.

He got on his knees, and with our translator's assistance, William gave his sins, hurts, and feelings of betrayal, rejection, and abandonment to the Lord. He told us he felt at peace after praying and felt something change in his emotions. Although William had not made a conscious decision to sign up for prayer again, the Lord somehow orchestrated the appointment for him and healed his heart.

Our Lord does relentlessly pursue us. He also gives us free will, so it is our choice to respond to His beckoning. Jesus does not force Himself upon us. He will provide us with the strength we need to face each day.

Have you not known? Have you not heard? The LORD is the ever-lasting God, the Creator of the ends of the earth. He does not faint or grow weary; his understanding is unsearchable. He gives power to the faint, and to him who has no might he increases strength. Even youths shall faint and be weary, and young men shall fall exhausted; but they who wait for the LORD shall renew their strength; they shall mount up with wings like eagles; they shall run and not be weary; they shall walk and not faint. (Isaiah 40:28–31)

Only Seek Truth from God

Several people told us they or their family members sought relief for their pain and suffering by seeking advice from fortune-tellers and psychics, rather than asking God to intervene. They did not realize that this, unfortunately, opened a door for darkness to enter their lives. Unbeknownst to them, these practitioners aligned themselves with Satan's supernatural forces. In 1 Samuel 28, we read that Saul turned to an occult medium before his tragic downfall.

The Bible clarifies that we should not look to people who practice divination, tell fortunes, act as mediums, or speak to the dead because these are abominations to the Lord. (See Deuteronomy 18:10–12.) We need to turn to the Lord for everything, and He will guide our paths. Psalm 32:8 says, "I will instruct you and teach you in the way you should go; I will counsel you with my eye upon you."

Out of desperation, several men at the prison told us their families contacted occult practitioners to request healing and release from the intense emotions plaguing them daily. They were often afflicted with feelings of extreme fear, rejection, anger, addiction, and unworthiness. Although some of their families professed to be Christians and attended church regularly, they sought help from witch doctors, voodoo specialists, and fortune-tellers for their relatives. Often this involved paying money to the person who claimed they could heal broken hearts and illnesses or cast spells on people perceived to be causing distress to their loved one.

After their initial meeting and payment for services, the practitioner required the afflicted person to complete elaborate rituals at home. To guarentee healing, the practitioner demanded more money. Instead of receiving the peace they sought, the person experienced more fear. They indicated they did not receive protection and instead felt threatened with great harm if they stopped paying the spiritualist.

During inner healing prayer, they forgave the occult specialists and their relatives, who mistakenly thought seeking wisdom and healing through occult practices would help them. The men renounced their part in believing these lies and asked the Lord for forgiveness for opening this door to the enemy. Ties with the occult and evil spirits were renounced and severed. The men asked the Lord to fill them with His Holy Spirit, and they received His blessings for their lives. We often heard them say they felt freedom and release from oppression. Their countenance also changed, and they looked calmer and peaceful. Again, the Lord set the captives free.

We offered several practical suggestions for the prayer recipients to follow to maintain their freedom. We knew the enemy would try to steal their peace and tempt them to seek comfort from the occult again. They needed to stand firm and declare all connections with the occult are severed. We explained that the enemy would try to convince them he has the truth, but he takes a kernel of truth and then twists to deceive his followers. Only God has the truth. The following suggestions were offered:

1. We encouraged them to fellowship with other Christians who could mentor and encourage them in their walk with the Lord.

2. We shared that praying with the Lord throughout the day and listening for His response is vital. They may experience the Lord's response as a thought in their mind, a picture or vision, a dream, words from another Christian, or a Bible passage.

3. We clarified the Bible reveals God's truth. Whenever they doubt something, even a response from another Christian, they need to

see if it lines up with what the Bible says. If it does not align with God's Word in the Bible, they need to discard it.

4. Joining a Bible study with other Christians would foster their spiritual growth as they sharpen each other and hold each other accountable.

5. Giving God control over their lives and trusting Him with their future leads to the freedom they desired. Entanglement with the occult leads to fear and torment.

6. When they find themselves taking back their burdens, repent and return the problems to Jesus. He will receive them and never let them down.

Pray this prayer aloud:

Lord, help me to daily turn all my burdens over to You. It is comforting to know that nothing that happens to me is a surprise to You. I stand on Your promise in Romans 8:28 that You will cause everything to work for good for those who love You and are called to Your purpose. You alone are my strength and refuge. Forgive me when I have sought others for the truth and safety. You are the only source of truth and protection. I want the freedom and peace only You can provide. Amen.

SECTION 8

Final Thoughts

You do not need to wait until you get to Heaven to experience all the Lord has for you. He has more for you right now. Lean into Him daily through conversation and prayer. Expect to hear from Him and see miracles. When you rest in Him each day, you will become aware of His active role in your life.

CHAPTER 23

Next Steps

Have you experienced hurt and pain and wondered where do you go from here? How can this distress amount to anything beneficial?

God did not cause the adverse events, but He can use them for good—your good and also for the benefit of others. You may hear people who have experienced abuse or trauma ask, "How can a loving God allow this to happen to me?" Remember, we live in a fallen world.

Often, the enemy causes suffering. Our God is a gracious and loving Father who wants to redeem us. God does not waste our pain. Joseph experienced horrific tragedy after his brothers sold him into slavery. In Genesis 50:20, Joseph says to his brothers, "As for you, you meant evil against me, but God meant it for good, to bring it about that many people should be kept alive, as they are today."

Finding an inner healing prayer or deliverance ministry may be the next step. Ask the Lord in prayer to guide you in your search for prayer ministers who can facilitate your restoration. If you belong to a church, ask if it has a healing prayer ministry. If it does not, ask your pastor or church leaders to suggest several organizations that offer these ministries. Organizations such as Christian Healing Ministries (CHM) and Restoring the Foundations (RTF) have trained people worldwide on healing prayer.

These training centers may suggest people in your local area that have completed their coursework and can provide healing prayer. Some organizations offer prayer through Zoom when meeting in person with a trained prayer minister is not possible.

Do not underestimate the power of forgiveness. It is the beginning of your healing, even if the offender's heart remains hardened. You are not responsible for the offender's response. They may not know that you forgave them. Your decision to forgive is essential to your restoration. Remember, you may not feel like letting the person who hurt you off the hook, but you do it as an act of obedience to the Lord. Ask the Lord to help you forgive those who harmed you.

Healing can happen instantaneously, but emotional healing is often a process. Do not be discouraged if you do not sense restoration immediately. The Lord often peels wounds off layer by layer. He tells us in the Scriptures that His burden is light. He will not overwhelm you. You can trust His timing regarding your healing.

After the Lord has removed several layers of wounding and you experience His peace, consider asking Him how you can partner with Him to help restore others who have experienced similar wounding. Warren writes, "Your *greatest* ministry will most likely come out of your greatest hurt."[1] You must be willing to share your painful experiences with others so God can use your wounds to heal others. Who better to help someone dealing with a difficult situation than someone who has been there and received Jesus's touch and restoration? He did this for me, and He can do this for you.

Based on the Scriptures, Warren believes God will ask us two critical questions when we stand before Him. First, He will ask, "What did you do with my Son, Jesus Christ?" Your answer will define where you spend eternity. Then, He will ask, "What did you do with what I gave you?" Your response will determine what you do in eternity.[2] How would you answer these questions?

Do you have an intimate, personal relationship with Jesus? If you do not, invite Him into your heart now. It is as simple as first believing in the

Lord and then receiving from Him. He is waiting to lavish His love on you. Confess your sins and ask for His forgiveness. He has already promised to forgive your sins if you sincerely confess them. Next, invite Jesus to transform your mind and cleanse you. Your prayer does not need to use elaborate words. It can be as simple as saying, "Help me, Jesus. Change me to be more like You." Surround yourself with healthy Christians who have a personal relationship with Jesus to help mentor you. Remember, it is not too late to turn your life over to the Lord. If you are still breathing, it is not too late.

Now that you have sought the Lord, you may wonder how you will know that you are hearing from Him. He still speaks to us today, but we often do not recognize His voice amidst the world's distractions. We need to tune out the distractions. God speaks to us through the Scriptures. The Bible is still relevant for our teaching today and can guide your life. Over time, as you interact with the Lord in daily conversation, you learn to recognize how He relates uniquely to you.

When I hear from the Lord, it is often an inner voice in the form of a thought or a word. You may question if the idea is your own. As you draw closer to the Lord, you will recognize His promptings. If what you are hearing does not align with His Word in the Bible, it is possible it is not from Him and is from the enemy. Seek the company of other Christians who have walked with the Lord and are familiar with His voice. They can speak into your life. Again, make sure what you are sensing and what others share with you aligns with God's character and His Word. The Holy Spirit will convict you of the truth, but He does not condemn you. Condemnation is from the enemy.

You may also see something from the Lord in a vision or a dream. The Bible contains numerous stories of God speaking to His people through dreams and visions. Sometimes you feel a conviction of right and wrong. Other times, people describe an impression or discernment they know is the Lord. Others feel an unexplainable peace. Jesus said that His followers would know His voice. The more you draw close to the Lord, the more you will learn and recognize Him speaking into your life. He will guide you in your destiny and His purpose for your life.

The Holy Spirit gives each person spiritual gifts to be used in the service of others to encourage, buildup, and comfort. (See 1 Corinthians 12 and Romans 12.) Do you know what your spiritual gifts are? If you are unsure, think about the areas you gravitate toward that provide joy. Where is your passion directed? The answers to these questions can provide clues to your talents. Some assessments can assist in determining your spiritual gifts. Press and I completed inventories that suggested our spiritual gifts in two churches where we were members. These surveys prompted us to consider ministry areas where we might serve using our abilities. Ask the Lord to highlight the spiritual gifts He gave you. Other Christians also can speak into your life and describe what they see as your strengths.

We get the privilege of telling others about Jesus and helping them discover their destiny. Jesus gave us the Great Commission when He said in Matthew 28:18–20, "All authority in heaven and on earth has been given to me. Go therefore and make disciples of all nations, baptizing them in the name of the Father and of the Son and of the Holy Spirit, teaching them to observe all that I have commanded you. And behold, I am with you always, to the end of the age." We do not necessarily need to travel overseas to evangelize and tell others about Jesus. Some people receive this calling. We can all reach others in our communities and families and witness Jesus's love by the way we lead our lives and care for each other daily.

You wonder why God placed you within your specific family. We heard people question this, especially when they endured challenging family relationships. There are no perfect parents. We do not have God's perspective, so we may not understand why He put us in the family He selected. Nevertheless, God does not make mistakes. Trust Him to show you what He wants you to learn through your family connections. Do you need to forgive them? Do you need to forgive yourself for dishonoring your relatives? If the relationships are toxic, you may need to set boundaries. Ask the Lord to bring people into your life who can guide your next steps.

We need to decide now if we will continue to live for ourselves or God. If you have not already committed to serving the Lord, you need to believe God loves you and has a purpose for your life. You are not an accident, even if you may have been a surprise to your parents. You were not a surprise to God. Read Psalm 139 to learn more about how well God knows you and loves you.

Live your life from the perspective of eternity. Ecclesiastes 3:11 tells us God put eternity into our hearts. He wants you to be with Him forever. If we start living with eternity in the forefront, this will color how we handle every situation. Our life on earth is the training ground for when we will spend the rest of our lives in the presence of God, Jesus, and the Holy Spirit. Heaven is your home. Do not let problems discourage you. Reframe them as opportunities to learn something new from the Lord and to develop your character. Ask the Lord for a lens change so that you can see the difficulties the way He sees them.

According to the Scriptures, we have many blessings to look forward to in eternity. Remember, we will live with God forever and become transformed like Jesus. There will be no pain, death, or suffering in eternity. We will be rewarded and given positions of service by the Lord, and we will share in God's glory. No one can take this priceless inheritance from us. You do not need to wait until you get to Heaven to start experiencing an abundant life with the Lord. You can expect miracles now.

EXPECT MIRACLES:

- Examine your motives and desires. Are there priorities, agendas, or relationships that need to change for you to be in sync with your new relationship with the Lord? Have you identified any open doors to the enemy that need closing? Are there any unhealthy generational patterns or soul ties that need breaking? Are there any lies that need renouncing? If so, use the prayers in the earlier chapters to guide you. Our manual *Simple Effective Prayer: A Model for Inner Healing* also provides specifics on inner healing.

- X marks the spot. Understand that God placed you on earth at this appointed time for a divine purpose. You are in the right place and time. If you are unsure of your destiny, ask the Lord. He designed you for a reason.

- **Problems are not your focus.** God is bigger than any difficulty you face. He has all the answers. Remember, God sent an angel to give Jesus strength in the Garden of Gethsemane before His crucifixion. He will comfort you in your suffering. As you draw closer to the Lord, you can expect to encounter more attacks from the enemy. Do not be discouraged. The enemy is worried that you will walk into your destiny, and he will attempt to thwart that.

- **Enjoy God's glory.** You can see it in nature and the beauty all around you. Look at the expanse of the universe. His glory can be seen in His Son, Jesus Christ, who came to earth so we could more fully grasp God's magnificence. Take time to appreciate the wonder in our world. Then, give God glory through your praise and worship and by loving and serving others.

- **Continually talk with the Lord.** Daily conversation is key to sustaining your relationship with Him. The seventeenth-century French monk, Brother Lawrence, knew the essential ingredient in a Christian's life is to stay in the Lord's presence. He showed the reader how to practice daily talking to God. In *Practicing the Presence of God*, Brother Lawrence humbly and simply described how even commonplace menial tasks could be acts of praise and worship to God.[3] Imagine everyday tasks such as washing dishes and preparing meals as devotion to the Lord. Brother Lawrence's words, written more three hundred years ago, are still applicable today. We need to change our attitude toward what we do rather than changing what we do.

- **Tell others about Jesus.** Describe your relationship with Him. Others will see the change in you and want to know what happened and why you carry peace. Matthew 5:14–16 tells us we are the light of the world, and we need to let that light shine for others to see.

- **Miracles do happen.** We saw countless times when the Lord healed emotional and physical wounds for the people who came to us for prayer. Our God is in the business of healing and miracles.

If you would like to learn more about inner healing, consider reading *Simple Effective Prayer: A Model for Inner Healing*. We used that model to pray with hundreds of people who experienced healing, peace, and the Lord's presence. Perhaps one of the greatest miracles of all is that when we accept Jesus as our Savior, He promises us eternal life. In John 10:28–29, Jesus said, "I give them eternal life, and they will never perish, and no one will snatch them out of my hand. My Father, who has given them to me, is greater than all, and no one is able to snatch them out of the Father's hand."

- **I**nvest in others. Love others with your God-given gifts. Mark 10:45 tells us that Jesus "came not to be served but to serve, and to give his life as a ransom for many." Jesus showed us how to be servants. We become more like Jesus when we follow His example. When we invest in others, we take the focus off ourselves. Our problems are then no longer our focal point.

- **R**est in the Lord and receive His peace. Ask the Lord to show you how to rest. Often, we are focused on doing rather than being. Our identity as sons and daughters of the Lord is more important than what we do. Take time each day to listen to the Lord by seeking Him during your quiet time. We need to shut out the noise of the world so that we can hear from the Lord. Jesus modeled this for us when He went up on the mountain away from the crowds to pray alone. (See Matthew 14:23.) We also know that apart from the Lord, we can do nothing. (See John 15:5.) We need to quiet ourselves and sit in God's presence daily.

- **A**cknowledge your need for God. Ask Him to show you what He is teaching you when you face challenges. These difficulties may be opportunities for you to learn something that you would not have had the chance to do otherwise.

- **C**hurch family is essential. Fellowship with other Christians. We often heard Christians tell us that other Christians wounded them.

Do not let this discourage you from meeting with other Christians. Ask the Lord where He would like you to connect with others.

- Laugh and enjoy life. Proverbs 17:22 says, "A joyful heart is good medicine, but a crushed spirit dries up the bones." Take time to refresh yourself. If you keep giving yourself to others without taking the time to refill your emotional tank, you will run dry. You cannot share what you do not have.

- Experiences are for sharing. Be willing to reveal your painful memories and the problems you faced to help others. God can use your life experiences, even those you are not proud of, to benefit others. He will not waste your hurts.

- Seek God. Often, we pursue the goosebumps and joy we feel when worshipping. Yet, we need to desire the giver of miracles, the Lord, not just the beautiful experiences. The magnificent encounters are an added blessing. It is essential to cry out to the Lord when you experience pain and heartache. He will empower, guide, protect, and comfort you. Only the Lord can give you the freedom you desire because He is the source of all good things.

Pray this prayer aloud:

> Lord, I want to walk in the destiny You have for me. Sometimes, I am unsure of the next steps. Your Word in Philippians 1:6 assures me that "he who began a good work in you will bring it to completion." I trust You to guide each of my steps and use my hurts for good as we partner together in healing. Help me to lean into You each day. Give me wisdom. When the enemy attempts to harm me, remind me whose child I am. I am Your precious, redeemed child. Thank you for adopting me into Your family. Amen.

Appendix

Negative	Ancestral	Influences
Abandonment	Depression/hopelessness	Perfectionism
Abuse (emotional/mental)	Failure	Pornography
Abuse (physical)	False guilt	Poverty
Abuse (sexual)	Fears	Pride
Abuse (spiritual)	Freemasonry	Rebellion
Abuse (verbal)	Gender identity issues	Rejection
Addiction	Grief	Religion (legalism)
Anger/rage	Hatred	Sexual sin/perversion
Anxiety	Idolatry/false religion	Shame
Bitterness/criticalness	Loss	Sleep issues
Bound emotions	Mental health issues	Suicidal thoughts/attempts
Chronic illness/infirmity	Neglect	Torment/confusion
Control issues	New Age involvement	Trauma
Condemnation	Occult (witchcraft)	Unbelief
Cult involvement	Oppression	Unworthiness
Death	Orphan lifestyle	Victimization
Deception/lying	Performance-oriented	Violence

Notes

Introduction

1   The website for Christian Healing Ministries; https://www.
    christianhealingmin.org
2   Randy Clark, *There is More! The Secret to Experiencing God's Power to
    Change Your Life* (Bloomington, MN: Chosen Books, 2013).

Section 1: Darkness

Chapter 1: Darkness Can Take Hold, but Don't Fear

1   R. T. Kendall, *How to Forgive Ourselves-Totally* (Lake Mary, FL:
    Charisma House, 2007), 117.
2   Jake Kail, *Keys for Deliverance: Freedom from the Influence of Evil Spirits*
    (www.jakekail.com, 2018), 69.
3   Frank Hammond, *Demons & Deliverance in the Ministry of Jesus*
    (Plainview, TX: The Children's Bread Ministry, 1991), 5–8.
4   Commentary in Jack Hayford, executive ed., *NKJV Spirit-filled Life
    Bible-* 3rd ed. (Nashville: Thomas Nelson, 2018), 1720.

Section 2: Open Doors

Chapter 2: Sin, Trauma, and Unforgiveness

1   Jake Kail, *Keys for Deliverance: Freedom from the Influence of Evil Spirits*
    (www.jakekail.com, 2018), 67.

2   Rick Warren, *The Purpose Driven Life: What on Earth Am I Here For?* (Grand Rapids, MI: Zondervan, 2002), 54–55.

3   Sharon Jaynes, *"I'm Not Good Enough" . . . and Other Lies Women Tell Themselves* (Eugene, OR: Harvest House, 2009), 172–173.

4   Derek Prince, *They Shall Expel Demons: What You Need to Know about Demons-Your Invisible Enemies* (Grand Rapids, MI: Chosen Books, 1998), 106.

5   Prince, *They Shall Expel Demons*, 106. Used with permission from Chosen Books, a division of Baker Publishing Group.

6   Kail, *Can a Christian Have a Demon?* (www.jakekail.com, 2014), 52.

Chapter 3: Ancestral Influences

7   Jake Kail, *Keys for Deliverance*, 74.

8   Marilyn Hickey (2000). *Breaking Generational Curses: Overcoming the Legacy of Sin in Your Family* (Tulsa, OK: Harrison House, 2000), 40.

9   Prince, *They Shall Expel Demons*, 210. Used with permission from Chosen Books, a division of Baker Publishing Group.

10   Marilyn Hickey and Sarah Bowling, *Blessing the Next Generation: Creating a Lasting Family Legacy with the Help of a Loving God* (New York: Faith Words, 2008), 59, 19.

Chapter 4: Word Curses

11   Bernie Siegel, *Love, Medicine & Miracles* (New York: HarperPerennial, 1998), 29.

12   Francis and Judith MacNutt Training Center, *School of Healing Prayer: Level II* (Jacksonville, FL: Christian Healing Ministries, 2008), 49–54.

Chapter 5: The Occult

13   Andy Reese and Jennifer Barnett, *Freedom Tools: Revised and Expanded Edition.* Bloomington, MN: Chosen Books, 2015), 171.

14   Reese and Barnett, *Freedom Tools*, 172.

15 Robert L. D. Cooper, *Cracking the Freemasons Code: The Truth About Solomon's Key and the Brotherhood* (New York: Atria Books, 2007), 204.

16 Jack Harris, J. (1983). *Freemasonry: The Invisible Cult.* (New Kensington, PA: Whitaker House, 1983), 62, 60, 51.

17 John Salza, *Masonry Unmasked: An Insider Reveals the Secrets of the Lodge.* Huntington, IN: Our Sunday School Visitor, 2006), 116–19.

18 Salza, *Masonry Unmasked,* 189–191.

19 Derek Prince, *Blessing or Curse: You Can Choose.* (Grand Rapids, MI: Chosen Books, 1990), 24–27.

Chapter 6: Soul Ties

20 Bill Banks and Sue Banks, *Breaking Unhealthy Soul-Ties* (Kirkwood, MO: Impact Christian Books, 2011), 16.

21 David Cross, *Soul Ties: The Unseen Bond in Relationships.* (Lancaster, England: Sovereign World, 2006), 63.

22 Banks and Banks, 62, 58.

23 Signs of an unhealthy soul tie are paraphrased from Kris Vallotton, "7 Unhealthy Signs of a Soul Tie," [Web Log Post], May 3, 2019, https://www.krisvallotton.com/7-signs-of-an-unhealthy-soul-tie

24 Banks and Banks, 122.

25 Side effects of unhealthy soul ties are paraphrased from Banks and Banks, 113–115.

Section 3: Forgiveness

Chapter 7: Understanding Forgiveness

1 Rodney Hogue, *Forgiveness* (Abilene, TX: Rodney Hogue Ministries, 2008), 27.

2 John Hopkins Medicine, "Forgiveness: Your Health Depends on It" The John Hopkins University, the John Hopkins Hospital, and the John Hopkins Health System. https://www.hopkinsmedicine.org/health/wellness-and-prevention/forgiveness-your-health-depends-on-it, 2020.

3   Kendall, *Revised and Updated Total Forgiveness*, 72, 84.

4   Kendall, 138.

5   Hogue, 13. Used with permission from Rodney Hogue.

Chapter 8: Benefits of Forgiveness

6   Kendall, 100–103.

Chapter 9: Releasing Ourselves and God

7   R. T. Kendall, *How to Forgive Ourselves-Totally* (Lake FL: Charisma House, 2007), 27.

Section 4: Lies

Chapter 11: Generational Patterns and Shame

1   Sharon Jaynes, *"I'm Not Good Enough"* . . . *and Other Lies Women Tell Themselves* (Eugene, OR: Harvest House, 2009), 15, 29, 37, 51. Used with permission from Harvest House.

Section 5: Emotional Wounds

Chapter 13: Your Feelings Aren't Right or Wrong

1   Bryn Farnsworth, "How to Measure Emotions and Feelings (And the Difference between Them)," (blog), *Imotions*, April 14, 2020, https://imotions.com/blog/difference-feelings-emotions.

Chapter 14: Guilt

2   R. T. Kendall, *How to Forgive Ourselves-Totally* (Lake FL: Charisma House, 2007), 33.

Chapter 15: Fear

3   Leif Hetland, *Healing the Orphan Spirit-Revised Edition* (Peachtree City, GA: Global Mission Awareness, 2013), 37, 79.

Section 6: God is in Control

1   Paul Simon and Art Garfunkel, vocalists, "I Am a Rock," Recorded December 14, 1965 and released January 17, 1966 on *Sounds of Silence*, Columbia Records, 33 1/3 rpm. https://www.youtube.com/watch?v=JKlSVNxLB-A

Chapter 18: You Are Not Alone

2   Twila Paris, "God is in Control," 1995. https://www.lyrics.com/track/1931818/Twila+Paris/God+is+in+Control
3   Chester Kylstra, "Escaping the Orphan Lifestyle." MP3 audio download produced by Restoring the Foundations, 2013. https://rtfresources.org/escaping-the-orphan-lifestyle-mp3-download/.
4   Kylstra, "Escaping the Orphan Lifestyle."
5   Chester Kylstra, "Understanding the Orphan Lifestyle." MP3 audio download produced by Restoring the Foundations, 2007. https://rtfresources.org/understanding-the-orphan-lifestyle-mp3-download/.
6   Kylstra, "Escaping the Orphan Lifestyle."

Section 7: Nothing Can Separate You from God's Love

Chapter 20: It's Not Too Late

1   Randy Clark, *Power to Heal: Keys to Activating God's Power in Your Life.* (Shippensburg, PA: Destiny Image, 2015), 12, 13.

Chapter 21: You Can Depend on God

2   Philip Yancey, *Disappointment with God.* (Grand Rapids, MI: Zondervan, 1988), 24, 36.

3   Yancey, *Disappointment with God.* 200–01.

Chapter 22: God is Bigger Than Our Problems

4   Rick Warren, *The Purpose Driven Life: What on Earth Am I Here For?* (Grand Rapids, MI: Zondervan, 2002), 173.

5   Warren, *The Purpose Driven Life: What on Earth Am I Here For?*, 195.

Section 8: Final Thoughts

Chapter 23: Next Steps

1   Rick Warren, *The Purpose Driven Life: What on Earth Am I Here For?* (Grand Rapids, MI: Zondervan, 2002), 246–47. Used with permission from Zondervan.

2   Warren, *The Purpose Driven Life*, 34. Used with permission from Zondervan.

3   Brother Lawrence, *The Practice of the Presence of God with Spiritual Maxims* (Grand Rapids, MI: Spire Books, 1967), 30.

simple
effective
prayer

FINDING FREEDOM
and inner healing

The Simple Effective Prayer (SEP) inner healing prayer model is focused on emotional healing and removing the ways that a person is hindered from developing a healthy connection with the Father, Son, and Holy Spirit. The model seeks to help a person by removing negative ancestral and soul tie influences, by replacing false beliefs with truth, and most importantly, healing heart wounds. Our website https://simpleeffectiveprayer.com has information and videos on the prayer model and how to learn to pray with others for healing. The SEP manual and support material will be available exclusively on the simpleeffectiveprayer.com website.

Author's Note

Thank you for reading *Freedom from Brokenness*. I pray you were blessed and will share this book with others. My husband Press has written a series of novels on healing prayer and spiritual warfare that you will find both entertaining and enlightening.

The first book in the *Freedom in Healing* series is *The Awakening*. This is a short novel about people from a traditional church becoming aware of healing prayer and how they can learn to help others. A free copy of *The Awakening* is available through our website: https://simpleeffectiveprayer.com. Provide your email address and we will send you the e-book, as well as occasionally update you with new information. Email addresses will not be shared or sold for any reason.

We pray you will enjoy *The Awakening* and will purchase the first full-length novel in the *Freedom from Healing* series titled *The Battle*. You can purchase *The Battle* from Amazon.com or request a copy from your favorite bookstore. If you have questions or want a signed copy of any of our books, please contact us at sepprayer@yahoo.com.

Press and I ask that if you buy a copy of any of our books on Amazon.com, that you would consider posting a review.

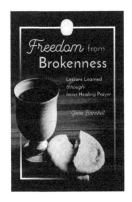

Made in the USA
Middletown, DE
17 March 2023

26972672R00116